Welcome to

# BUTTERMILK
# KITCHEN

*Welcome to*

# BUTTERMILK
# KITCHEN

## SUZANNE
## VIZETHANN

PHOTOGRAPHS BY **Angie Mosier**

**GIBBS SMITH**
TO ENRICH AND INSPIRE HUMANKIND

## Dedication

*For my dad, Ray, who taught me the most
important things you need to have in life:
happiness, a good dog, and great food.
This book is for you!*

First Edition
24 23 22 21 20        5 4 3 2 1

Text © 2020 Suzanne Vizethann
Photographs © 2020 Angie Mosier

Published by
Gibbs Smith
P.O. Box 667
Layton, Utah 84041

1.800.835.4993 orders
www.gibbs-smith.com

Designed by Michelle Farinella
Printed and bound in China
Gibbs Smith books are printed on either recycled, 100% post-consumer waste, FSC-certified
papers or on paper produced from sustainable PEFC-certified forest/controlled wood source.
Learn more at www.pefc.org.

Library of Congress Cataloging-in-Publication Data
Names: Vizethann, Suzanne, author. | Mosier, Angie, photographer.
Title: Welcome to Buttermilk Kitchen / Suzanne Vizethann ; photographs by Angie Mosier.
Description: First edition. | Layton, Utah : Gibbs Smith, [2020]
Identifiers: LCCN 2019037891| ISBN 9781423653462 (hardcover) |
ISBN 9781423653479 (epub)
Subjects: LCSH: Cooking, American—Southern style. | Buttermilk Kitchen (Restaurant) |
LCGFT: Cookbooks.
Classification: LCC TX715.2.S68 V58 2020 | DDC 641.5975—dc23
LC record available at https://lccn.loc.gov/2019037891

Buttermilk Kitchen has a special feel to it; you know it when you walk through the door. It's a charming and cozy space filled with the aroma of warm biscuits, buttery grits, and crispy fried chicken. Outside of these perfectly executed comfort-food standards, however, there's much more to discover on the pages of this cookbook. Think beet-cured lox, homemade jams, creative salads, and very opinionated egg recipes. Suzanne Vizethann has a knack for making the kind of food we all crave, and it's now been captured within the binding of her first book. As you sift through the recipes, your mouth will water and your cast iron skillet will rattle to be freed from the cupboard.

—Steven Satterfield, James Beard award-winning chef and restaurateur

You don't see too many quintessential breakfast concepts, but what Suzanne has created with her restaurant Buttermilk Kitchen is the exception. She's a force in the kitchen, she cooks from the heart, and has the ability to transform something simple into something exceptional. Her passionately sustainable kitchen methods are inspiring to the industry and will continue to declare her as someone the community can count on. I cannot wait to try Suzanne's biscuits at home!

—Chef Anne Quatrano, James Beard award-winning chef and restaurateur

I knew from the first few moments working with Suzanne that she was destined for success. Welcome to Buttermilk Kitchen provides great insight and access to her vision, and the recipes will finally give her fans the ability to cook some of her favorite recipes for themselves. A must-have cookbook for the collector and beginner alike.

—Chef Richard Blais, chef, restaurateur, cookbook author, and television personality

What can I possibly say about Suzanne and Buttermilk Kitchen that has not already been said by countless fans of hers, who line up bright and early every morning vying for a warm cup of coffee and one of her famous biscuits? I can tell you that in the number of times I have dined with her, I have always tried a new dish and not been disappointed. I can tell you that every time we have cooked together, she has wowed diners with her inspired interpretations of Southern classics. I can also tell you that her story is one of true grit (pardon the pun) and determination, and that I am thrilled to finally learn how to make some of her most memorable dishes. Maybe now I can sleep in a little later and make her Pimento Cheese Omelet with Bacon and Red Pepper Jelly on my own at home; or maybe I just prefer to have her to continue to make them.

—Chef Kevin Gillespie, chef, restaurateur, and cookbook author

# CONTENTS

# *Foreword*

As you make your way down Roswell Road, just outside of Buckhead, Atlanta, you might not even notice the quaint little house that's set just enough off the road to possibly escape your attention. Despite its signature brilliant blue paint job and its charming flower boxes, the exterior of Buttermilk Kitchen doesn't exactly give you the impression that you are about to eat at one of Atlanta's finest restaurants. You won't be greeted by some hipster valet, the restaurant itself wasn't put together by some cutting-edge design firm, and each menu item isn't served on its own unique piece of china. In fact, upon making your way into the space, you're more likely to feel as if you're about to eat at a friend's house, because Buttermilk Kitchen feels like home—home to well over 2,000 folks per week.

No reservations or call-aheads are taken. On most days, you will likely be greeted by a ridiculously long wait. The line often spreads throughout the parking lot. The folks you see equipped with umbrellas on rainy days and sipping big cups of Starbucks coffee have been here before. From 8 a.m. to 2 p.m., Tuesday through Sunday, Buttermilk Kitchen is simply a machine. If you're a first timer, do yourself a favor: dine by yourself so that you can sit at the counter. But if you're bringing someone to dine with, make sure that person isn't very tall, because if they are, there's a good chance they'll feel like they're dining in a doll house, sitting at tables that came out of their kid's kindergarten classroom. Buttermilk Kitchen isn't exactly spacious, and if you think the dining room is a tight squeeze, you should have seen the first incarnation of its kitchen—you would have thought the Keebler Elves were cooking your breakfast. But nonetheless, some folks probably wouldn't even mind sitting on milk crates out back, mauling those ridiculously delicious biscuits while enjoying the view of the dumpsters.

Alright, you waited about an hour for a table—not bad. Next time, try coming out on a Wednesday morning, and if you get here just after 10 a.m., you'll slide right into the sweet spot and you'll be devouring a pimento cheese omelet or a market scramble within fifteen minutes of arriving. It could have been worse—trust me. Imagine waiting for a table for well over an hour *without* the help of alcohol; it almost sounds inhumane. That's how it was for the first five years. Now the booze is flowing at BK, and everyone is welcome to catch a buzz while they wait for a table.

So you're finally at a table and you're checking out the menu, as well as the plates of the guests on either side of you, and you take notice of a girl who looks like she just walked off the set of an Ivory Soap commercial. She's making her way through the dining room, greeting folks with her piercing smile and her youthful looks. No, that's not your server, and she's not wearing her brother's oversize kitchen shirt. No, that's not the owner's daughter—that's the owner, and she's the chef, too. Folks, allow me to introduce you to the "girl next door," Suzanne Vizethann.

This humble house that is a restaurant, the girl who looks like she just graduated from college or just returned from backpacking through Europe, and all of the other ancillary and insane charm that encompasses an average trip to Buttermilk Kitchen makes you almost feel taken advantage of or emotionally manipulated. It's all a setup made to make you order more biscuits or a bottle of red pepper jelly to go. You couldn't have scripted anything better. You can't make this up.

There's no denying that Buttermilk Kitchen has established itself as one of the finest dining establishments in all of Atlanta, if not the entire Southeast. A place such as Buttermilk Kitchen is the perfect instrument for progress within the food community because its raw energy excites people; it inspires them to share their individual food experiences, thus paving the way for continued growth within both realms of cooking,

professional and personal. Buttermilk Kitchen's approachable and unpretentious manner is ironically what makes it the dynamic force that it is within Atlanta's dining community. Moreover, it's able to welcome both walks of life, those looking for an experience and those just looking for a plate of properly cooked soft scrambled eggs.

My reason for coming is simple—Buttermilk Kitchen, in its purest form, truly represents Suzanne Vizethann: the woman, the chef, and the diner. I enjoy "seeing Suzanne" throughout BK's entire body, whether it's a specific song on the playlist, a new piece of artwork hanging in the dining room, or a dish featuring Suzanne's newest food obsession. Buttermilk Kitchen's infrastructure has been fortified with countless layers of substance, because Suzanne conceived a specific vision for Buttermilk Kitchen. She instilled this vision within her staff, and her staff has helped share this vision with literally thousands of people who have dined at Buttermilk Kitchen. Suzanne has crafted, almost as an art form, an eatery that perfectly balances certain nuances and amenities of a fine dining restaurant with the comfort and sensibilities of home cooking and the overall charm of a general store.

Now for some of the bad nitty-gritty. You didn't think it was all rainbows and unicorns for Suzanne, did you? Nope. There were a lot of tears, a lot of no-shows, and just a whole lot of stuff that Suzanne simply didn't know going into this project. Not to mention that the building was literally a dump, and the kitchen had an industrial steel pole that stood squarely in the middle of the hot line. Hopefully Suzanne will commission me to write the entire story of Buttermilk Kitchen one day, but until then, let's just say that there are very few pleasant surprises when you're opening a restaurant. Being the chef and the owner is like a double homicide, and once you get to the point where the sound of your name drives you to utter madness, you know things are just getting warmed up. Owning and operating a restaurant is a lot like having a kid: just because you can, doesn't mean you should. It is a labor of love, and sometimes a thankless endeavor, that many days owns you. Of course, after a few dozen meltdowns and just a few years, Suzanne quickly started figuring all this out. Buttermilk Kitchen was running like an actual restaurant. The widespread panic that once ran wild throughout each shift had been replaced with the perfect balance of competence, passion, and dysfunction.

I've given Suzanne a lot of advice over the past decade, and when she chooses to take it, she usually does so at least a year or so after the fact. But if you ask her which piece of advice has proven to be the most valuable, and the piece of advice that she took almost instantly, I think Suzanne would bring up the conversation that she and I had late one night, after yet another dreadful day on the ranch. Suzanne is not used to not doing well. In fact, Suzanne

simply does not *not* succeed. The early days of Buttermilk Kitchen were simply miserable for her. She was emotionally and physically spent: the restaurant business had thus far been beating her up and it was not about to stop. That's the scary part of all of this. After you wash off one day's filth and tribulations, in a matter of hours, it's time for more. All of the problems that you thought you left behind on Wednesday are still lurking around on Thursday. And there are more problems to go with it.

The idea that every day is a clean slate or a new beginning is utter bullshit. Save your naïve positivity for your next Instagram post. The produce delivery is still late, the hostess still doesn't understand that seating the entire dining room at once is actually a bad thing, and you remember the cook that couldn't cook an over-medium egg without breaking the yolk yesterday? Well, that problem just got a bit more complicated. His dreams of becoming a chef and owning his "own little fifty-seat place" were crushed by yesterday's chaos and confusion, and today the thought of that insurance adjuster position his friend mentioned to him is looking pretty appealing, and guess what? He didn't show up. You know how you make it all stop, at least temporarily? Close the crazy place for a day. Done. Wow—that felt good. We should do this next Monday, too. Really? We can do that? Yep, it's one of the very few perks of being the owner. And that's the best advice I ever gave Suzanne. Buttermilk Kitchen is not open on Mondays.

You know what Suzanne's best attribute is? She is extremely patient. You know what Suzanne's greatest flaw is? She is ridiculously impatient (and stubborn). Suzanne truly is a prodigy. When she embarked on opening Buttermilk Kitchen, she didn't have nearly enough experience to run her own place, she didn't have enough money, and she didn't have enough money. But she did have a clear vision of what Buttermilk Kitchen was going to be and what she was going to get out of it. She refused to concede to the traditional notions and ideas of what a restaurant has to be and how it has to be operated. If there's one dated and archaic sentiment that pervades the restaurant industry, it's that everyone has to pay their dues and follow a certain sequence of steps before embarking on their own journey. Everyone has to be patient, and wait for his or her rite of passage. Suzanne completely ignored this notion and continued down her path on her own terms. Why doesn't Buttermilk Kitchen serve dinner? Simple: Suzanne doesn't want to work at night. For as open-minded and creative as I am, this revelation of not being open for dinner has always been stunning to me. But who am I to judge? I'm the one writing the foreword for her book—not the other way around.

What's the perfect example of Suzanne's patience? I've eaten countless biscuits at Buttermilk Kitchen and I have never tasted or detected the slightest inconsistency in any of these biscuits. Her willingness to tweak, adjust, and tweak a recipe, time and time again, is the defining testament to her passion for food. So I guess you're in for a treat with this book.

I'd like to say that I am impressed Suzanne has written a cookbook, but I am not. And quite frankly, neither is she. I'm actually surprised it took this long for her to do it. While Suzanne has surely approached this project with the same zeal and enthusiasm in which she does most everything, this cookbook is just another example of Suzanne getting things done. Suzanne likes making lists and crossing items off those lists. And then she makes another list. If I know Suzanne, while this cookbook is just another logical part of her ever-evolving career and brand, it's also simply a genuine and vibrant way for Suzanne to share her ideas and love of food. Although most of Suzanne's primal energy is indeed rooted in logic, she is an artist. Her art is food, and nothing brings her more fulfillment than watching all walks of life consume her art. I urge you to not simply enjoy these recipes, but appreciate how Suzanne is able to masterfully blend the notion of cooking in a practical and sensible manner with the creative exploration of all the possible boundaries of any dish or ingredient. If fully and properly digested, this book will serve all of us well and remind us how important it is to do something as simple as share a meal with one another.

—Ron Eyester,
The Angry Chef

## Acknowledgments

I am fortunate to have an amazing support system and family. Without them, this book wouldn't be possible.

To every employee (good or bad) who has ever worked for me, and especially the original warriors: Evan, Crystal, Kurtis, Juanie, and Winnie. Thank you for grinding it out for me on those hot summer days with no air conditioning in the kitchen. I could not do this without you, and I am truly thankful for each and every one of you.

To my crazy girlfriends: Addie, Brittany, Anna, Katie, and Liz—my ride or die homies. I am so fortunate to have such a strong group of females to call my besties. You have all been there for me since the beginning days. I am sorry for all the birthday parties, weddings, and other lifetime achievements I missed.

To my friends and family who have supported me throughout these years—thank you for continuing to eat at Buttermilk Kitchen. I am lucky to have you.

To Richard Blais and Sandra Bank for giving me my start in this crazy industry. I don't know if I should thank or blame you! Nonetheless, I appreciate you taking a chance on me.

Angie Mosier, my dear friend and photographer—these beautiful photographs wouldn't have been possible without you. It was your support and wisdom that guided me through this book. Looking forward to our second one!

Conor, this would not be possible without you, simple as that! Thank you for always believing in my dream, having my back, and looking out for my best interests. You are my sister and the best person I know.

To all the chefs who have inspired me and let me stage for them—you remind me why I love this profession. You know who you are.

Ryan, my incredibly patient boyfriend who keeps me smiling every day. Thank you for taste testing these recipes—it was a hard job, but someone had to do it.

To my mom and sister for always believing in me and being by my side. I love you both so much. We are going to do that business together one day!

To our wonderful vendors for supplying us with amazing ingredients. I truly could not have done this book without you.

To Ron for continuously talking me off the ledge and believing in me. Where would I be today without our long talks on the drives to Tennessee? Thank you for showing me how brunch is done, and for letting me know when I play too many notes. It's all happening!

To Veronica and Lioba for teaching me how to cook, and for recipes I will cherish forever.

To all of our customers, regulars, #buttermilkbabies, and Yelpers. Thank you for your continued support, honest feedback, and for staying on this journey with us.

To Annette, Janice, and Laura for your insight and assistance in making this book become a reality. It's been a long time coming!

And to Dad. Life hasn't been the same without you. Thank you for helping me turn my dream into a reality. I hope you are looking down and that this book makes you proud.

# Introduction

Open a restaurant, they said. It will be fun, they said! This business can be far from fun at times, but truth be told, it's the only thing I've ever been truly passionate about.

This is how I became Mrs. Buttermilk.

To me, nothing signals the start of a good day more than the sound of bacon sizzling in a cast-iron skillet, or the sight of a just-broken yolk oozing into the nooks and crannies of a piece of warm, buttered toast. My name is Suzanne Vizethann. I'm a born and bred Southerner, chef, and restaurant owner. I paid homage to my roots by opening Buttermilk Kitchen in my native city of Atlanta, Georgia. You may be thinking, "How neat," but in reality, I was two months shy of my thirtieth birthday and had no idea what the hell I was doing.

Although I had paid my dues, or so I thought, by graduating from culinary school and staging for a handful of top chefs in Atlanta and New York City, starting a restaurant from scratch was far more challenging than I ever could have imagined. When Buttermilk opened, I wore many hats and worked ninety-hour weeks. I was exhausted all the time and practically lived at the restaurant. Despite the grueling hours and early challenges, there were two critically important things that kept me going—my passion for cooking never wavered, and my commitment to only using fresh, local ingredients set Buttermilk apart.

"Buttermilk" refers to the liquid utilized after butter is churned, carrying out the philosophy of letting nothing go to waste. This concept is how I first came up with the name for the restaurant. Well, and the ring of Buttermilk Kitchen is undeniably Southern.

My mission has always been to delight customers with refined Southern breakfast and lunch dishes, several of which are from my childhood. There are more dinner-focused restaurants opening in Atlanta every month than I can count on two hands. Not to knock on them, but I wanted to create something simple, sophisticated, and unique. Something that resonates with everyone, from discerning foodies to home cooks and everything in between. One reason I wrote *Welcome to Buttermilk Kitchen* is to encourage home cooks to reconsider the opportunities that morning meals present. The ingredients are often found as close as your pantry or the neighborhood farmers market.

Throughout this book, you will learn to cook dishes that put Buttermilk on the map. A customer favorite is the fried Chicken Biscuit (page 76) that's brined in sweet tea (see page 35) and fried in day-old pancake batter (see page 37). Here in the South, it's perfectly acceptable to eat fried chicken for breakfast. In fact, it's encouraged. Another staple dish is Ray's Waffle Burger (page 119), which is a tribute to my dad. You will learn the full story of this recipe later, but it originally came to fruition because my dad ran out of bacon one morning when I was a small child.

Our menu is less inspired by current crazes and more by timeless traditions. My Italian grandmother, or Nonna, as we all called her, thought of cooking as an art—an opportunity to find beautiful ingredients to prepare a dish with love over the course of several hours. I have carried on this tradition at Buttermilk by making nearly everything from scratch, the way I would for loved ones at home. We beet-cure our lox in-house (see Beet Lox Cure (page 49)), lending it a distinctive pink glow. Our house pickles and jams use produce from local farmers and we squeeze our own juice.

For years, there has been a lot of interest in how we do things at Buttermilk Kitchen. Customers inquire about our recipes, want to buy our homemade jams, or want to learn how to make our biscuits. Ultimately, people want to recreate the dishes they wait in long lines for week after week. My hope is to empower readers to make delicious, company-worthy food in their own homes, and, of course, to have fun while doing it. I want to share the lessons I have learned along the course of my exhilarating culinary journey. My greatest honor as a chef is to share the magic of Buttermilk Kitchen with homes around the world. From our kitchen to yours!

# OUR PANTRY

People always ask, "How do you get your pancakes so fluffy, your biscuits so crunchy, and your eggs so creamy?" The secret is in the ingredients we use—great ingredients equal great food. It can be challenging to charge a premium at breakfast, a meal commonly undervalued, but sourcing high-quality eggs should be just as important as the chicken served at your dinner table.

This section is meant to show you the ingredients we use and how we source them, as well as educate you on the proper way to handle them. If you pay a premium for your products, you need to treat them with care.

I understand that you may not always have access to these ingredients, so it's okay to make substitutions. Just remember these recipes are written using the following list, and if you need to swap one out, keep in mind that the flavor and integrity could be altered. When in doubt, use the best tool available to you—your taste buds!

## Bacon

We use two types of bacon at Buttermilk Kitchen: Allan Benton's Hickory Smoked Country Bacon (https://shop.bentonscountry ham.com/) and Hormel natural thick cut and smoked bacon. We use Benton's bacon to balance sweet dishes or to make our bacon fat, as it is very smoky. For side dishes and sandwiches, we use Hormel.

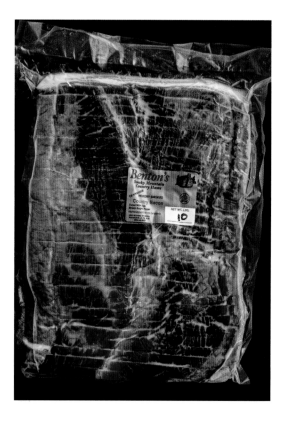

## Black Pepper

We buy whole black peppercorns and grind them fresh. This is a critical step and will make all the difference in your recipes. Grinding peppercorns is easy to do with a coffee grinder or peppermill. If you do not have access to either one of those, buy the peppercorns that already come in their own cracker. Store your ground peppercorns in a container with a tight-fitting lid at room temperature, and only grind small amounts at a time. Pepper will keep for several years, but the flavor is best when it's ground fresh.

## Bread

All of the bread we use is delivered daily from a local bakery, H&F Bread Co. (hfbreadco.com). We use their Southern white bread, multigrain bread, and Jerusalem bagels.

## Butter

We use a lot of butter, as it is a very important ingredient. We always use unsalted butter, and so should you—you have better control of seasoning in your recipes. For all of our baking recipes, we use Wüthrich Unsalted European-style butter, which has 83% butter fat (compared to domestic butter at 80%) and allows a higher smoking point. We use Banner Butter's (http://bannerbutter.com/) Unsalted Cultured Butter for finishing (to top our pancakes, on the side of a biscuit, etc.), as we want you to actually taste the flavor of the butter. If we are clarifying butter (see page 47), we will use a more generic, store-bought product.

## Buttermilk

If you can't tell by our name, buttermilk is obviously a very important ingredient to us. All of the buttermilk at the restaurant is from Banner Butter, a local butter company about thirty minutes up the road from us. All of the cream used to make their butter comes from pasture-raised Georgia cows, resulting in an awesome flavor.

## Cornmeal and Oats

We use finely-ground yellow cornmeal and stone-cut oats from Anson Mills, which lies just down the road from my alma mater, University of Southern California, in Columbia, South Carolina. I can't say enough about Anson Mills. Their website alone provides you with enough research material to earn a culinary degree in grains. I have never tasted oats so good, and they are critical in our oatmeal recipe (page 126). I strongly encourage you to purchase your grains from their retail website before proceeding with any recipes calling for oats or cornmeal. For recipes that call for rolled oats, like our Granola (page 129), we use organic old-fashioned rolled oats.

## Eggs

All of the eggs used at the restaurant are from Handsome Brook Farms (handsomebrookfarm.com). The eggs are pasture raised, meaning the hens graze on grass and are allowed plenty of room to roam outside. Hens that eat and live

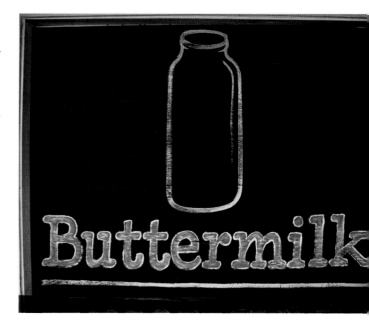

outside lay eggs that generally taste better than hens that do not. Happy hens equal happy eggs. If you are unable to find Handsome Brook Eggs at your local grocery store, buy eggs from a farmer at your local farmers market or another high-quality, pasture-raised brand.

## Flour

We only use one type of flour at the restaurant, and that is King Arthur Unbleached All-Purpose Flour milled from American wheat. It is a very versatile ingredient—strong enough for dredging fried chicken, and tender enough for pancakes and biscuits. Store flour in a container with a tight sealable lid away from direct sunlight. Your flour should keep for at least six months or several years in the freezer.

## Grits

Our grits come from Logan Turnpike Mill in Blairsville, Georgia. We use their old-fashioned, speckled white grits (https://loganturnpikemill.com/old-fashioned-speckled-white-grits/), which are ground on stones. Seek out stone-ground grits, which are much coarser than traditional grits and yield a creamy texture. We store all of our grits in an airtight container in the freezer.

## Honey

We use raw honey from the Little Bee Project (see page 60) in Atlanta. Sourcing local honey should be easy enough and readily accessible at your local grocery store. Always look for it in its raw form, as the health benefits are endless.

Raw honey has a better taste, aroma, and color that will enhance your recipes.

## Meat

We use all-natural, preservative-free meats at the restaurant and source them from farms that humanely treat their animals. Our chicken is ordered from Coleman Natural or from Joyce Farms in North Carolina. Our sausage is from Pine Street Market and Delia's Chicken Sausage Stand in Atlanta, Georgia. Our ground beef is always grass fed and sourced from Painted Hills Natural Beef in Oregon.

## Maple Syrup

Ok, I hate to admit it, but I grew up eating Aunt Jemima syrup on my pancakes. When I first tried real maple syrup, I did not like the taste. It was almost too strong for me—I was used to all of that corn syrup and genetically modified sugar found in the store-bought brands. As I tasted it more, I began to understand how much better the maple flavor was when found in pure syrup. It is more robust and will make your pancakes, or anything else you put it on, sing. The syrup at Buttermilk Kitchen is 100% pure and comes from Little Man Syrup in Wisconsin. If you are buying maple syrup from the store, look for a label that says "pure" and does not include the word "blend." Store syrup in an airtight container on your shelf or in your refrigerator to extend the life. Alternately, you can freeze it for up to one year.

## Nutmeg

We grind nutmeg fresh every day. It's much fresher and tastier than ground nutmeg and makes all the difference in your recipes. Try it in our Classic French Toast batter (page 95) or grate it into your morning coffee.

## Oils

We use a couple different oils at the restaurant. For frying, dressings, and mayos, we use a non-GMO neutral canola oil. For salad dressings, we use a high-quality olive oil, and for finishing, we use Agrumato Lemon Oil.

## Salt

We use two types of salt—Maldon, which is a high-quality sea salt we use for finishing, and Diamond Crystal Kosher Salt, which we use for everything else. Salt is a very important ingredient, if not the most important, when it comes to cooking. Salt enhances the natural flavors in food, so you want to use a good brand when cooking. Salt lasts forever and is a fun thing to collect. Make it more exciting by adding herbs or fruit zest to it. Always store it in an airtight jar in your pantry.

## Sugar

We use granulated sugar for all baking recipes, which is important in the creaming stage. We also use light brown sugar and confectioners' sugar (powdered sugar) for topping pancakes or making rubs. For recipes where you can actually taste the sugar, we opt for turbinado sugar for its robust, almost molasses-like flavor.

## Vinegar

Vinegar is an amazing ingredient and brings brightness to dishes. It is key when poaching eggs (see page 111) or pickling fruits and vegetables (see page 38). We use a rotating variety, but you will most commonly find white, balsamic, and cider on our shelves.

# EQUIPMENT

Equipment is just as important as the ingredients you use. If you want to be successful in creating our recipes, you need to consider the equipment you have on hand. We source most of our smallwares from WebstaurantStore.com, which is like Amazon for restaurants.

## Blenders, Mixers, and Grinders

*Blender* We use a commercial Vita-Prep blender for most everything that we do—however, they are extremely expensive. Not that I am trying to talk you out of the investment, but any high-powered blender will do just fine in our recipes. We also use an immersion hand blender, which is useful when making jams, soups, and gravy.

*Food processor* We use a commercial food processor in our kitchen called a Robot Coupe, which can be expensive. You will just need a basic one, like the Cuisinart 4 Cup or the Breville Sous Chef.

*Grinder* These are essential for grinding your own spices or coffee. We use a basic Cuisinart coffee grinder, which comes with different size settings.

*Stand mixer* The KitchenAid 5 Quart Stand Mixer is, in my opinion, one of the best kitchen investments you can make. It comes with every attachment under the sun, but the three standards we use are the paddle, whisk, and dough hook.

## Blow Torch

Not only are blow torches fun, they are inexpensive. We use them to caramelize our bananas (see page 102), but they have several other uses. They act as your own portable broiler. I would purchase from your local hardware store or online. You will commonly see them advertised as a crème brûlée torch, but I prefer the heavy-duty Bernzomatic.

## Containers

We use plastic food pans with airtight lids to store all of our prepared food. It is important that they always have an airtight lid on them—you don't want them picking up other scents in the refrigerator. Can you imagine strawberries left out next to your minced onions? Not the best flavor combo when you're trying to enjoy a fruit bowl. For larger prep projects, like our house pickles, we use Cambro 4- and 8-quart non-reactive polycarbonate food containers.

## Cooking Gear and Serveware

*Box grater* I am pretty sure everyone has one of these in their home kitchen, but you're probably not used to hearing it called by that name. A box grater is essential for grating cheese and butter for our O.G. Buttermilk Biscuit recipe (page 59).

*Ice cream scoops* You would think we run an ice cream shop when you see the amount of ice cream scoops we use. They are a vital tool when shaping our biscuits (see page 59) or achieving roundness in our buttermilk pancakes (see page 92). The most common sizes we use are 1-ounce, 2-ounce, and 4-ounce scoops. I could give you alternate tools to use instead, but it won't be the same. So go ahead and add them to your Amazon cart now.

*Silicone pastry brushes* These brushes are great for finishing baked items with melted butter or coating bread with olive oil.

*Slotted and perforated spoons* These are great when you need to stir sauces or drain meats. The holes allow grease to drip from the food, which makes it a great tool when frying.

*Spatulas and turners* These are super important when stirring and flipping ingredients. We use turners and fish spatulas for flipping meats and pancakes and heat-proof silicone spatulas for almost everything else.

*Steak weights* These weights are great for achieving a good sear or crust on meat. They act as a weight to press down your food and can even speed up the cooking time of our Classic French Toast (page 95).

*Tasting spoons and stirrers* Any chef will tell you that spoons are an essential part of any kitchen, and I am no different. I love a good spoon and have one in every size. They are great for stirring, serving, and tasting. The sizes I most commonly use are a tablespoon, a $2\frac{1}{2}$ tablespoon, a Gray Kunz spoon, and teaspoons.

*Tongs* Tongs are made to make handling and cooking foods easy. We use heavy-duty, stainless steel 7-inch, 10-inch, and 12-inch ones.

*Whisks* Whisks are always a great tool to have on hand for combining ingredients. Buy stainless steel and get a couple different sizes.

## Gloves

Gloves are not only important for the health inspector, they're an easy way to keep your hands clean. Gloves serve their purpose when they need to, but sometimes you should rely on your bare hands to properly handle an ingredient, like when making our Pimento Cheese Spread (page 82) or when seasoning. If you aren't using gloves, make sure your hands are clean and your fingernails are trimmed and free of dirt.

## iSi whipper

A lot of people fear the iSi whipper, which is really just a fancy whipped cream dispenser. Remember those Reddi-wip cans? That is essentially all an iSi whipper is, you just have to load it yourself. It makes whipped cream in

an instant and allows for creativity and beautiful presentations. My favorite iSi whipper can be purchased from webstaurantstore.com. Make sure you have CO2 chargers to fill your dispenser, which you can also purchase from Webstaurant. You'll want to buy the cream chargers instead of the soda ones.

## Knives and Cutlery

*Chef's knife/all-purpose knife* This is the most important type of knife to have in the kitchen. A lot of chefs geek out when it comes to their brand of knives, but the two most important things to remember when picking out your knife is that it should feel good in your hand and be kept sharp. Dull knives are way more dangerous than sharp ones. I use a MAC Santoku 6.5-inch chef's knife that I have had since culinary school.

*Mandolin* Mandolins are great for slicing fruits and vegetables with precision. You don't have to have one of these, but if you are not skilled with a knife, I would highly suggest it. Just remember to watch your fingers!

*Microplane* This is a must-have tool that is highly underutilized in the home kitchen. They are used most commonly to zest fruits or grate nutmeg, which is an amazing way to add flavor to dishes.

*Paring knife* These are great for peeling and chopping smaller items, such as fruit and vegetables.

*Serrated knife* These knives have a saw-like edge and are essential for slicing breads, bagels, and other soft products. Do not use these knives for anything else. They have their purpose and should stick to that.

## Ladles

These are great for serving and measuring; we use them to portion our pancakes. I would suggest having a 2-ounce, 4-ounce, and 6-ounce size in your kitchen.

## Measuring Vessels

*Mason jars* I use this as my standard measuring cup at home. I like to use the 16-ounce-wide or regular jar. Just make sure you buy the one that has the measurements written on the side of the glass. These jars are also great for storing prepared items, like Reggae Grits (page 143).

*Measuring cups* It's good to have two clear liquid measuring cups on hand: the 2-quart and 2-cup capacity. Then get a four-piece dry measuring cup set that includes the $1/4$ cup, $1/2$ cup, $3/4$ cup, and 1 cup.

*Measuring spoons* You will also want a four-piece set that includes the $1/4$ teaspoon, $1/2$ teaspoon, 1 teaspoon, and 1 tablespoon.

## Mixing Bowls

Stainless steel mixing bowls are inexpensive, stackable, and a kitchen must. I buy them in all different sizes, but you will need a small ($1 1/2$-quart), a medium (3-quart to 4-quart), and a large (8-quart).

## Pots and Pans

*Cast iron* I could write a whole book on cast iron cookware. They are great for searing, baking, sautéing, or frying. The maintenance on them requires a little effort, but I couldn't live without one. For our recipes, you will need a 10-inch or 12-inch skillet, such as a Lodge.

*Nonstick frying pans* These pans are what we cook all of our eggs in. You will need an 8-inch and 9-inch or 10-inch pan.

*Saucepans* Saucepans are a solid investment and can make all the difference in your cooking. You will need a 4-quart to 6-quart and an 8-quart capacity stock pot for our recipes. Look for pots made by All-Clad or that are stainless steel or enamel. Aluminum pans, while inexpensive, are highly reactive and can alter the foods flavor and appearance. I personally love Calphalon or Le Creuset.

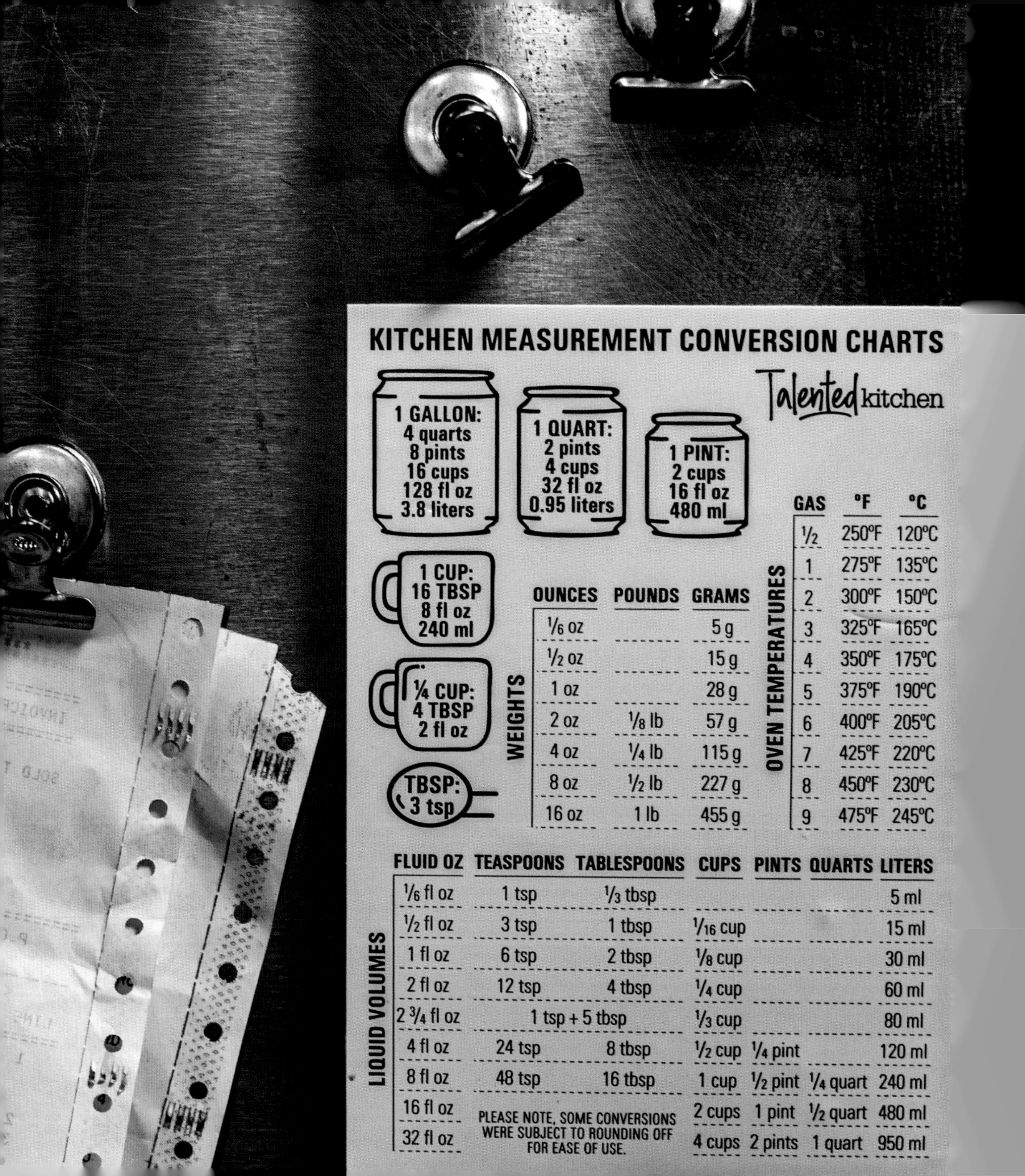

# KITCHEN MEASUREMENT CONVERSION CHARTS

*Talented* kitchen

**1 GALLON:**
4 quarts
8 pints
16 cups
128 fl oz
3.8 liters

**1 QUART:**
2 pints
4 cups
32 fl oz
0.95 liters

**1 PINT:**
2 cups
16 fl oz
480 ml

**1 CUP:**
16 TBSP
8 fl oz
240 ml

**¼ CUP:**
4 TBSP
2 fl oz

**TBSP:**
3 tsp

## OVEN TEMPERATURES

| GAS | °F | °C |
|-----|------|------|
| ½ | 250°F | 120°C |
| 1 | 275°F | 135°C |
| 2 | 300°F | 150°C |
| 3 | 325°F | 165°C |
| 4 | 350°F | 175°C |
| 5 | 375°F | 190°C |
| 6 | 400°F | 205°C |
| 7 | 425°F | 220°C |
| 8 | 450°F | 230°C |
| 9 | 475°F | 245°C |

## WEIGHTS

| OUNCES | POUNDS | GRAMS |
|--------|--------|-------|
| ⅙ oz | | 5 g |
| ½ oz | | 15 g |
| 1 oz | | 28 g |
| 2 oz | ⅛ lb | 57 g |
| 4 oz | ¼ lb | 115 g |
| 8 oz | ½ lb | 227 g |
| 16 oz | 1 lb | 455 g |

## LIQUID VOLUMES

| FLUID OZ | TEASPOONS | TABLESPOONS | CUPS | PINTS | QUARTS | LITERS |
|----------|-----------|-------------|------|-------|--------|--------|
| ⅙ fl oz | 1 tsp | ⅓ tbsp | | | | 5 ml |
| ½ fl oz | 3 tsp | 1 tbsp | 1/16 cup | | | 15 ml |
| 1 fl oz | 6 tsp | 2 tbsp | ⅛ cup | | | 30 ml |
| 2 fl oz | 12 tsp | 4 tbsp | ¼ cup | | | 60 ml |
| 2 ¾ fl oz | 1 tsp + 5 tbsp | | ⅓ cup | | | 80 ml |
| 4 fl oz | 24 tsp | 8 tbsp | ½ cup | ¼ pint | | 120 ml |
| 8 fl oz | 48 tsp | 16 tbsp | 1 cup | ½ pint | ¼ quart | 240 ml |
| 16 fl oz | | | 2 cups | 1 pint | ½ quart | 480 ml |
| 32 fl oz | | | 4 cups | 2 pints | 1 quart | 950 ml |

PLEASE NOTE, SOME CONVERSIONS WERE SUBJECT TO ROUNDING OFF FOR EASE OF USE.

## Scales

It's always best to use a scale for accuracy, especially when baking. It's good to have a 5-pound mechanical portion-control scale, a digital gram, and an ounce scale.

## Strainers

Strainers are crucial in our kitchen. We most commonly use the chinois (shin-wah), or fine-mesh strainer, a china cap (larger holes), or a sieve for sifting flours and powders. To skim grits and oatmeal, we use a tea strainer.

## Thermometers

*Candy thermometers* are great for deep frying or cooking in high heat. They generally test up to 450 degrees F, compared to standard thermometers that top out at 212 degrees F.

*Digital instant-read thermometers* are great for testing internal temperatures when you do not want to cut into something. All our cooks are required to have one at their station. It improves accuracy and lowers the chance of foodborne illnesses.

## Timers

We have so many timers at the restaurant that it's hard to keep up with them. Timers are a great way to ensure even and accurate cooking time. You may have one on your cell phone, but I suggest you purchase a couple magnetic ones to have on your refrigerator.

# KITCHEN PLAYLISTS

Music is super important to set the mood in a restaurant. Although headphones are strongly frowned upon in the kitchen, I believe there should always be music playing, as it establishes the mood and overall identity of the restaurant. I personally cook better when there is a good playlist going, and I always stress to my managers that they also have a good playlist on throughout the restaurant. Here are some of our Spotify playlists you can find playing on any given day at Buttermilk Kitchen. For more, follow us on Spotify at Buttermilk7 or feel free to make us some new playlists!

## SPANDEX (80s) MIX

*Let's Go Crazy* by Prince

*Bette Davis Eyes* by Kim Carnes

*Father Figure* by George Michael

*Oh Sherrie* by Steve Perry

*Dancing in the Dark* by Bruce Springsteen

*Gloria* by Laura Branigan

*Footloose* by Kenny Loggins

*Cream* by Prince

*99 Red Balloons* by Nena

*I'm So Excited* by The Pointer Sisters

*Borderline* by Madonna

*The Promise* by When in Rome

*King of Wishful Thinking* by New Found Glory

*Dance Hall Days* by Wang Chung

*The Best* by Tina Turner

## SOUL MIX

*I Got a Woman* by Ray Charles

*Pullin'* by Aretha Franklin

*Living for the City* by Stevie Wonder

*Lucille* by Little Richard

*Working My Way Back to You* by The Spinners

*Groove Me* by Etta James

*I Wish It Would Rain* by The Temptations

*I Shall Be Released* by Marion Williams

*The Rubberband Man* by The Spinners

*Will It Go Around in Circles* by Billy Preston

*Inner City Blues* by Marvin Gaye

*Sweet Soul Music* by Arthur Conley

*Get on the Good Foot* by James Brown

*California Dreamin'* by Bobby Womack

## REGGAE MIX

*Kaya* by Bob Marley

*Red Red Wine* by UB40

*In the Dark* by Toots and the Maytals

*Mama Africa* by Peter Tosh

*One By One* by The Black Seeds

*Badfish* by Sublime

*Rudy, A Message to You* by Dandy Livingstone

*Jah Garden* by The Gladiators

*Satisfaction* by Ken Boothe

*Hey Jude* by John Holt

*Freedom Train* by Toots and the Maytals

*Beautiful Dancer* by Fred Fisher

*Rudy Got Soul* by Desmond Dekker

# STAPLES

The recipes in this chapter are the building blocks for all other recipes we create at the restaurant. It is very important for all cooks to master these recipes first before tackling any of the other recipes. Most of these recipes yield large quantities. You can easily cut them in half if you want, but they last a long time and are good basics for stocking your pantry or refrigerator.

# Minced Garlic

*We always have batches of minced garlic and onion in our cooler to build flavor in dishes. Preparing them ahead is a great time-saver. They will last up to one week in the refrigerator.*

*Makes 1 cup*

2 cups whole cloves garlic, peeled

Place garlic in a food processor and pulse for 20 seconds. Using a silicone spatula, scrape down the sides and pulse again for another 20 seconds. Garlic should be minced but not broken down into paste.

# Minced Onion

*Makes 2 cups*

1 whole white onion, peeled

Place onion on a cutting board and cut in half. Cut each half into 4 pieces, yielding 8 pieces total. Put onion pieces in a food processor and pulse for 20 seconds. Using a silicone spatula, scrape down the sides and pulse again for another 20 seconds. Onion should be minced but not broken down into paste.

# Sweet Tea Chicken Brine

*All of our fried chicken takes a bath in this brine before being cooked. All the chicken we fry in the restaurant is white meat, which tends to dry out quicker due to its low fat ratio. Brining is really important when you are cooking chicken—it helps the meat retain its moisture, and the tea in this recipe gives it a wonderful flavor. This recipe is good for up to 15 pounds of chicken and will last in the refrigerator for up to two weeks.*

*Makes about 6 quarts*

6 quarts brewed unsweetened tea, divided

1 cup granulated sugar

$1^1/_2$ cups kosher salt

2 to 3 dried bay leaves

1 tablespoon whole black peppercorns

2 lemons, cut in half

$^1/_4$ cup whole cloves garlic, smashed

1 bunch flat-leaf parsley

Place 3 quarts unsweetened tea in a large stock pot. Set pot on stove over high heat. As soon as tea starts to boil, remove from heat and set aside. While the tea is still hot, add sugar and salt and stir with a whisk until completely dissolved.

Place bay leaves and peppercorns into a coffee filter tied with butcher's twine and add to tea mixture. Pour tea mixture into an 8-quart, nonreactive container. Add remaining tea, lemons, garlic, and parsley.

Let mixture chill completely, remove the spice bag, and strain before using.

# Chicken Stock

*Any time I have leftover vegetable scraps or herbs, I see a stock opportunity. Any aromatics do well in a stock, and they are a great way to extract extra flavor from vegetable skins or scraps that you would normally throw away. Keep this stock on hand for soups, Reggae Grits (page 143), or Sawmill Gravy (page 65).*

*Makes about 1 gallon*

> 5 pounds chicken bones
>
> 1 large onion, quartered
>
> 2 carrots, peeled and cut in half
>
> 2 stalks celery, cut in half
>
> 2 to 3 sprigs of rosemary/thyme
>
> leftover herbs (optional)
>
> 2 bay leaves
>
> 4 to 8 whole black peppercorns
>
> 5 cloves garlic, peeled
>
> 2 gallons cold water

Place all ingredients in an 8-quart stock pot. Cook on high heat until you begin to see bubbles break through the surface of the liquid, about 10–12 minutes.

Turn heat down to medium low so that stock maintains a low, gentle simmer. Skim the scum from the stock with a spoon or fine mesh strainer every 10–15 minutes for the first hour of cooking and twice each hour for the next 2 hours. Add hot water as needed to keep bones and vegetables submerged. Simmer, uncovered, for 6–8 hours.

Strain stock through a fine mesh strainer into another large stock pot or heat-proof container, discarding the solids. Put in refrigerator to chill overnight.

The next day, all of the fat in the stock will have solidified to the surface. With a large spoon, remove solidified fat, trying to leave as much of the liquid in the container as you can, and discard fat. Store liquid in a covered container in the refrigerator for 2–3 days or in freezer for up to 3 months.

# Fried Chicken Dredge

This is the seasoned flour we dredge all of our chicken in before frying. We also use this dredge for our Fried Pickled Green Tomatoes (page 150). This recipe makes a good amount, but it will keep for at least a couple months. Store in an airtight container and use whenever you have the urge to deep fry in flavor.

*Makes 10 cups*

8 cups all-purpose flour

$1/3$ cup garlic powder

$1/3$ cup onion powder

2 teaspoons paprika

2 teaspoons cayenne pepper

2 teaspoons kosher salt

1 teaspoon ground black pepper

Pour all contents into a large mixing bowl and mix using a whisk for 2 minutes. Then mix for another 3 minutes with hands until fully incorporated. Place in an airtight container for storage.

# Fried Chicken Batter

This recipe plays a very important role in the crispiness of our fried chicken. The grill cook's job at the end of each day is to make this with the pancake batter leftover from the shift. It gets thinned out with milk, yielding a perfect consistency for coating chicken.

*Makes enough for 10 to 12 pieces chicken*

4 cups day-old O.G. Buttermilk Pancake batter (page 92)

$3/4$ cups whole milk

Pour batter into a mixing bowl. Add milk slowly while whisking until completely incorporated. Let mixture rest for at least 10 minutes before using, or put in the refrigerator for up to 2 days.

# House Pickles

*Pickles were always a staple in my house growing up. They are full of flavor, provide an awesome crunch, and make great garnishes to sandwiches. They are easy to make and will last up to one month in the refrigerator—everyone should make their own pickles!*

*Makes about 1 quart*

    2 pounds (about 8 to 10) medium
        Kirby cucumbers

    1 quart Pickling Brine (page 40)

Cut the cucumber into $1/8$-inch-thick slices and place in a large nonreactive bowl.

Pour brine in a large saucepan over high heat and bring to a boil. Once brine starts to boil, pour it over the cucumbers. Place a couple of small plates over cucumbers to weigh them down, ensuring they stay submerged in the liquid.

Place the cucumber mixture in a quart-size container, cover, and refrigerate for at least 1 hour.

# Pickled Green Tomatoes

*Makes about 1 quart*

    1 quart Pickling Brine (page 40)

    2 pounds green tomatoes

Cut the tomatoes into $1/8$-inch-thick slices and place in a large nonreactive bowl.

Pour brine in a large saucepan over high heat and bring to a boil. Once brine starts to boil, pour it over the tomatoes. Place a couple of small plates over tomatoes to weigh them down, ensuring they stay submerged in the liquid.

Place the tomato mixture in a quart-size container, cover, and refrigerate for at least 1 hour.

# Pickling Brine

*This recipe has a kick. We pickle our green tomatoes and cucumbers (see page 38) in this flavorful brine. It uses a lot of vinegar, so have a window open when you make it. This recipe will make enough for 4 pounds of vegetables and will last in the refrigerator for up to 1 month.*

*Makes 2 quarts*

4 cups white vinegar

2 cups cider vinegar

4 cups granulated sugar

1/8 cup dry mustard

1/2 cup kosher salt

1/2 tablespoon turmeric

1/8 cup red pepper flakes

1/8 cup fennel seeds

1/4 cup whole black peppercorns

Place all ingredients in an 8-quart stock pot. Place pot on the stove over high heat. As soon as the mixture starts to boil, remove from heat and stir with a whisk until sugar and salt are completely dissolved.

Using a china cap or a fine mesh strainer set over a 4-quart container, strain pickling liquid and discard seasonings. If not using right away, put in airtight container and chill in the refrigerator overnight.

# Citrus Balsamic Vinaigrette

*You can use any type of citrus here. Try blood oranges when in season, or substitute grapefruit for an extra zing. This is a great recipe to have in your arsenal and goes well with tomatoes, salad, and even fruit.*

*Makes about 2¹/₂ cups*

1 orange

¹/₂ cup balsamic vinegar

¹/₂ tablespoon kosher salt

1 teaspoon freshly ground black pepper

1 tablespoon Little Bee or local honey

1 teaspoon minced garlic (see page 34)

1 tablespoon minced onion (see page 34)

2 cups olive oil or canola oil

Using a microplane, zest orange and place zest in a small mixing bowl. Cut orange in half, juice it entirely, then add juice to zest.

Add orange mixture and all remaining ingredients except oil to a blender. Turn on low speed and mix until ingredients are blended together, about 1 minute. Increase speed to medium and slowly stream in oil until fully incorporated.

Pour into an airtight container and store in the refrigerator for up to 2 weeks.

# House Vinaigrette

*This is an incredibly easy vinaigrette to make and great to have on hand for salads.*

*Makes about 2 cups*

> 1 1/4 cup cider vinegar
>
> 1 tablespoon Rosemary Salt (page 53)
>
> 1/4 cup Little Bee or local honey
>
> 1/2 teaspoon freshly ground black pepper
>
> 1 lemon, zested
>
> 1 1/2 cups of olive oil or canola oil

Add all ingredients except oil to a high-speed blender. Turn to low speed and mix until ingredients are blended together, about 1 minute. Increase speed to medium and slowly stream in oil until fully incorporated.

Pour into an airtight container and store in the refrigerator for up to 2 weeks.

# Alabama Ranch

*This is a hybrid between Alabama white BBQ sauce and ranch dressing. We use this as a dip for our Fried Pickled Green Tomatoes (page 150).*

*Makes about 1 cup*

- $1/2$ tablespoon minced fresh dill
- $1/2$ tablespoons minced fresh chives
- 1 cup Mayonnaise (page 45)
- 2 tablespoons plus 1 teaspoon cider vinegar
- $1/2$ teaspoon kosher salt
- $1/4$ teaspoon garlic powder
- $1/4$ teaspoon onion powder
- $1/2$ teaspoon Worcestershire sauce
- $1/2$ teaspoon ground black pepper
- Pinch of cayenne pepper

Place all ingredients into a small mixing bowl and, using a whisk, mix together until fully incorporated. If not using right away, place in an airtight container and store in refrigerator for up to 1 week.

CLARIFIED
BUTTER

MAYONNAISE

BACON FAT

ALABAMA
RANCH

LEMON
MAYO

MAPLE
AIOLI

# Mayonnaise

*The first thing you need to know before attempting to make your own mayonnaise is the rule of oil and water (vinegar in this case). I am sure you are all familiar with the old proverb "oil and water don't mix." Well, it's true! Lucky for you, some chemist discovered years ago that if you stream oil very slowly into the water/liquid you are working with, it would in fact mix together and create an emulsion. Mayonnaise is made the same way, and once you have conquered it, you will feel very accomplished. Make sure you use a neutral oil here—you do not want your oil to add extra flavor to the mayonnaise.*

*Makes 4 cups*

  $1/2$ cup egg yolks

  $1 1/2$ teaspoons kosher salt

  $1/8$ cup cider vinegar

  $1/8$ cup white vinegar

  3 tablespoons turbinado sugar

  4 cups neutral oil, such as canola
    or grapeseed

Add egg yolks, salt, vinegars, and sugar to the bowl of a stand mixer fitted with the whisk attachment. Mix on the lowest speed for 1 minute.

Turn mixer to medium speed and slowly stream in oil until fully incorporated. Once all oil has been added, turn mixer to medium high for 1 minute.

Now pat yourself on the back; you just made your own mayonnaise! Place in an airtight container and refrigerate for up to 2 weeks.

# Lemon Mayonnaise

*I love lemon mayonnaise, and you can put it on almost anything. We slather toast with it for our signature B.E.L.T. sandwich (page 122)*

*Makes 1 cup*

> 1 cup Mayonnaise (page 45)
>
> 1 lemon, zested and juiced*
>
> Pinch of salt

Whisk together all ingredients in a small mixing bowl. Store in an airtight container for up to 2 weeks.

*I can't count how many times I have watched a cook zest citrus improperly. To do it successfully, use a microplane (see page 26) and move the lemon in one direction against the blades. Turn the lemon as you go and remove only the yellow part, leaving the white pith behind.

# Maple Aioli

*Aioli is really just a fancy word for mayonnaise and an opportunity to introduce flavors to the condiment. We serve this sauce with our Ray's Waffle Burger (page 119) at brunch.*

*Makes about 1 cup*

> 1 cup Mayonnaise (page 45)
>
> 1/4 cup maple syrup
>
> 2 tablespoons Worcestershire sauce
>
> 1/2 teaspoon ground mustard

Whisk together all ingredients in a small mixing bowl. Store in an airtight container for up to 2 weeks.

# Clarified Butter

*What is clarified butter anyway? Butter has a lot of milk solids in it. If you have already made our Mason Jar Butter (page 71), then you saw how the butter separates from the cream when shaking. Some of that cream remains in the butter, and when you melt it slowly, the milk solids separate, leaving you with clarified butter. Another way to think about clarified butter is that it is a more clear, natural butter with a much higher smoking point than regular butter, which makes it ideal when cooking at high temperatures. We cook all of our eggs in clarified butter.*

*Makes about 2 cups*

    1 pound (4 sticks) unsalted butter

Cut butter in 1-inch cubes and place in a small saucepan over medium-high heat.

Melt butter until white milk suds float to the top of surface. Continue to cook butter until it comes to a boil and milk suds become frothy. Lower heat slightly and continue to cook until milk suds break apart and sink to bottom of pan.

Once boiling has stopped, pour butter through a chinois or fine mesh strainer (see page 29) lined with a coffee filter into a heatproof container to remove browned milk solids. Let cool then transfer to an airtight container and refrigerate until ready to use. Clarified butter should keep for at least 6 months in the refrigerator.

# Bacon Fat

*Bacon fat, or any animal fat for that matter, is an amazing and simple way to introduce umami to a dish. You can cook eggs in it, sear a hamburger patty in it, or use it as a base for the most amazing Nashville Hot Griddled Cornbread (page 99). When making bacon fat, it's important you cook over very low heat to ensure you render off as much of the fat as possible. If you cook it too fast, your bacon will crisp and burn before the fat has a chance to leak out of the meat.*

*Ask your local butcher for bacon ends, which are primarily fat. If you can't find them, you can substitute 5–6 strips of raw bacon.*

*Makes about 1/2 cup*

- 1 pound raw Benton's bacon ends (see page 18) or other high-quality bacon

Heat a large cast iron skillet on low heat. Add the bacon ends and let cook for about 30 minutes, turning them occasionally with tongs or a fork.

When the bacon strips are browned and start to crisp, lift them out of the pan and place on paper towels to drain excess fat.

Pour the remaining fat from the pan into a Mason jar or any other glass jar with a lid. Place jar in the refrigerator. Once chilled the bacon grease will solidify to a slightly off-color white. When you cook bacon again, pull out the jar and add more of the excess fat to it, creating the most amazing bacon fat collection ever.

## SPICED BACON FAT

*Makes about 1 cup*

- 1 cup bacon fat, melted
- $1^1/_4$ teaspoons ground cayenne pepper
- 2 teaspoons chili powder
- $2^1/_4$ teaspoons kosher salt
- 2 teaspoons paprika
- 1 teaspoon garlic powder
- 1 teaspoon onion powder

Combine bacon fat and seasonings together in a small mixing bowl. Store in the refrigerator.

# Beet Lox Cure

*This is how our signature Lox Plate (page 133) gets its amazing color. We shred beets that penetrate the salmon, leaving the fish with the most beautiful purple color. It's like a salmon sunset.*

*Makes about 4 cups, enough for 1 side of salmon*

   2 to 3 medium red beets, washed

   1 cup granulated sugar

   3/4 cup kosher salt

Cut beets in half on a cutting board. Using the largest holes on a box grater, grate beets and place into a medium mixing bowl. Mix sugar and salt into beets. Use immediately.

# House Seasoning

*Our house seasoning coats everything from our Hashbrown Fritters (page 144) to our Biscuit Crackers (page 174). It's also a good accompaniment to chicken or red meat.*

*Makes 2 cups*

1 1/2 cups kosher salt

1/8 cup turbinado sugar

1 tablespoon and 1 1/2 teaspoons ground black pepper

1/3 cup garlic powder

1 1/2 tablespoons onion powder

1 tablespoon curry powder

1/4 cup paprika

1/2 teaspoon cayenne pepper

Place all ingredients in the bowl of a food processor and pulse for 30 seconds until thoroughly combined and color turns pink. If not using right away, place in an airtight container and set in the pantry.

# Coffee Rub

*We use this rub on our Ray's Waffle Burger (page 119), but it would be good on chicken, steak, or fried eggs. This will last about a month, so feel free to double it so you have it on hand. If grinding your own coffee, make sure to put your grinder on the coarse or French press setting.*

*Makes 1 cup*

1/4 cup coarse-ground coffee

1/4 cup chili powder

2 tablespoons paprika

1 tablespoon kosher salt

1/4 cup turbinado sugar

Place all ingredients into a small mixing bowl and, using a whisk, mix together until fully incorporated. If not using right away, place in an airtight container and set in the pantry.

# Rosemary Salt

*Herb salts are so easy to make and are a great way to introduce flavor to dishes. We use rosemary here, but this recipe would work just as well with thyme, oregano, sage, or lavender.*

*Makes about 1 cup*

　　3 sprigs fresh rosemary

　　1 cup kosher salt

Strip rosemary leaves by starting at the top of the stem and pulling down. Mince rosemary and put in a small mixing bowl. Add salt and mix with a whisk until rosemary is completely combined with salt.

Place rosemary salt in an airtight container. The salt acts as a preservative, so this will last at least 6 months to a year.

# Cracker Seasoning

*You will love this seasoning mix. We serve it on our Biscuit Crackers (page 174), but it also goes great on eggs, meat, or buttered toast.*

*Makes 1 1/2 cups*

　　1/4 cup House Seasoning (page 50)

　　1/2 cup white sesame seeds

　　1/2 cup black sesame seeds

　　1/4 cup whole fennel seeds

Mix all ingredients together in a small mixing bowl with a whisk. Store in a Mason jar with lid or any sealable container.

# BISCUITS

I did not have a Southern grandmother who taught me the secrets of dough-making as soon as I could see over the counter. However, I did have a family who believed in sharing meals together and a German nanny who had quite the repertoire of authentic recipes. Growing up with them taught me that food has the power to connect people and the ability to create lasting memories.

We sell a truckload of biscuits at Buttermilk Kitchen! We make drop biscuits versus the more traditional rolled and steamed biscuits. If you want to get toned arms, come work in our pastry department for a week; it will be the most affordable gym membership you've ever purchased!

We make it a priority to use high-quality ingredients in these biscuits, from European butter (see page 18) to our buttermilk.

After our biscuits come out of the oven, we brush the top with melted butter to give them a flavorful crunch.

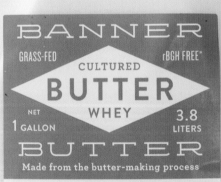

# BANNER

GRASS-FED                                    rBGH FREE*

CULTURED

# BUTTER

WHEY

NET                                            3.8
1 GALLON                                       LITERS

# BUTTER

## Made from the butter-making process

Butter Whey. Wait — Butter What? Rest assured. What you have in your hands is the real deal. Many years ago, when industrial-scale companies took over butter-making, they didn't "have time" to culture the cream before churning it into butter. They simply soured milk and called it buttermilk. But ours is the buttermilk you get when you churn real, true cultured butter. It's butter's milk. And that, friends, is Butter Whey.

Separation is normal.
Shake before using.

INGREDIENTS: Butter whey, live cultures

CONTAINS MILK
KEEP REFRIGERATED

**Nutrition Facts** Serving Size 1 Cup (240ml), Amount per Serving: Calories 150, Calories from Fat 70, Total Fat 8g (12% DV), Saturated Fat 5g (25% DV), Trans Fat 0g, Cholesterol 35mg (12% DV), Sodium 290mg (12% DV), Total Carbohydrate 12g (4% DV), Dietary Fiber 0g (0% DV), Sugars 11g, Protein 8g, Vitamin A (4% DV), Vitamin C (2% DV), Calcium (30% DV), Iron (0% DV), Percent Daily Values (DV) are based on a 2,000 calorie diet.

*The FDA states that no significant difference has been shown between milk derived from rBGH-treated and non-rBGH treated cows.

Banner Butter 3731 Northcrest Rd, Ste 3, Atlanta GA 30340        Plant 13-511

# BUTTERMILK

Great biscuits start with great ingredients, and all of our biscuits are made with Banner Butter buttermilk. I first met the owner of Banner Butter, Drew McBath, when we opened Buttermilk Kitchen in 2012. He was making delicious small-batch butter from the cream of grass-fed cows and selling it at the local farmers market. When he told me he wanted to sell the buttermilk, I thought "FINALLY!" Shortly after, we became the first restaurant carrying the product. We now buy eighty gallons a week of his delicious buttermilk, and we couldn't make those beautiful biscuits without it!

# O.G. Buttermilk Biscuit

*This is the biscuit that started it all and put us on the map. We make drop biscuits rather than rolled biscuits. If your biscuits do not come out the way you want them to the first time you make them, keep practicing. To make great biscuits is truly an art form.*

*Makes 10 (4-ounce) biscuits*

- 1 pound plus 1 stick unsalted European butter, frozen*
- 5 cups all-purpose flour
- 4 tablespoons granulated sugar
- 4 tablespoons baking powder
- 1 tablespoon plus 1 teaspoon kosher salt
- 2 3/4 cups Banner Butter buttermilk or other high-quality, full-fat buttermilk
- Melted butter (optional)

Preheat oven to 350 degrees. Prepare a half-size sheet pan with butter.

Grate frozen butter, using a box grater, onto a baking sheet lightly coated in flour, and then toss lightly with flour to coat.

Whisk together flour, sugar, baking powder, and salt in a large mixing bowl. Add in butter and fold into flour, mixing with your hands until mixture resembles sand. Add buttermilk and mix with your hands until dough comes together into a large ball (it should be soft and sticky).

Scoop biscuits, using a 4-ounce ice cream scoop or a 1/2 cup measuring cup sprayed with nonstick cooking spray, onto the sheet pan, leaving 1 inch between each biscuit. Bake for 10 minutes then turn and rotate pan and bake another 10–15 minutes. Check for color and doneness. The biscuits should be golden brown, crispy around the edges, and cooked in the middle. Brush immediately with melted butter.

*We freeze the butter for at least 30 minutes prior to making this recipe to make it easier to grate the butter.

**VARIATION**  To make honey biscuits, substitute raw honey for the sugar in the recipe.

# A STORY ABOUT HONEY

What could possibly pair better with biscuits than delicious honey? It's a match made in taste bud heaven. Growing up, my family was not keen on fast food, but occasionally you could find us heading to the drive-through line at KFC. I distinctly remember that my favorite thing to order was the biscuits with a side of honey packets. So when I opened Buttermilk Kitchen, sourcing good honey was a must.

I met Steve Esau in the early days of Little Bee Honey. He started making honey in his backyard in 2010. Being a farm boy from Kansas, he originally wanted chickens. His partner quickly gave a hard no on that, which led him into researching honey bees. He started with a couple hives, giving honey as gifts. His honey quickly gained popularity and has since grown into a profitable business with apiaries all over Georgia. The numbers on his labels correlate with the location of the apiary, as in #1025, which is what we use from Steve's backyard. The honey gets bottled and is in the restaurant 1–2 days later.

# Biscuit Croutons

*Biscuit croutons are a great way to utilize day-old biscuits. Try these on top of a salad for a nice crunch or use to garnish your favorite soup.*

*Makes about 4 cups*

> 3 to 4 day-old O.G. Buttermilk Biscuits (page 59)
>
> 1/3 cup olive oil
>
> 1 tablespoon Rosemary Salt (page 53)

Preheat oven to 400 degrees.

Working over a large bowl, tear each biscuit into 1-inch pieces to form the croutons.

Toss croutons with olive oil and salt to evenly coat then spread them out in a single layer on a half-size sheet pan. Use a second sheet pan as needed to prevent crowding, which will entrap steam and keep the croutons from browning.

Bake croutons for 5 minutes. Rotate the pans, switch the oven positions, and use a metal spatula to turn and rotate the croutons so that they brown evenly.

Bake the croutons another 5 minutes until they're golden brown and crunchy on the outside, with just a tiny bit of chew on the inside. Taste a crouton and adjust the seasoning with a light sprinkling of salt if needed.

Let croutons cool completely. Use immediately or keep in an airtight container for up to 2 days.

# BISCUIT ACCESSORIES

A biscuit is really just a blank canvas for endless combinations of spreads, butters, and jams. You can put most anything on a biscuit, but what follows are some of our favorites.

# Mushroom Gravy

*If you don't like "pork-on-your-fork," try this recipe. We are lucky enough to have an amazing mushroom producer, who grows lion's mane, oyster, and the most delicious chestnut mushrooms you will ever taste, at the farmer's market every Saturday. I think his chestnut variety produces the most flavor, but feel free to use any combination of your favorite mushrooms here. It's important to start with a really good vegetable stock as your base. I always recommend making it yourself—it's a great way to utilize vegetable scraps that you might normally throw away.*

*Makes 4 servings*

- $1/4$ cup minced onion (see page 34)
- 4 tablespoons unsalted butter
- 1 tablespoon minced garlic (see page 34)
- 1 cup chopped mixed lion's mane, chestnut, and oyster mushrooms
- 1 teaspoon salt
- Pepper, to taste

2 tablespoons all-purpose flour

$1/2$ cup vegetable stock

$1 1/2$ cups whole milk or nondairy milk of choice

Preheat a 4- to 6-quart saucepan over medium heat and begin cooking onion with butter. Once the onion is slightly amber, about 3 minutes, add garlic, continuing to cook for 1–2 more minutes, and then add mushrooms, salt, and pepper.

Gradually sprinkle in the flour while stirring. Once flour is incorporated, 1–2 minutes, begin adding vegetable stock while stirring. Increase heat to high and continue cooking until sauce comes to a boil and starts to thicken. Add milk and season with more salt and pepper if desired.

Pour over biscuits, toast, eggs, or just eat it by the spoonful!

# Sawmill Gravy

You won't get far on a southern breakfast table without Sawmill Gravy, meaning pork-based gravy. Be sure you grind the nutmeg yourself (see page 21), because it makes a big difference in taste. This recipe generates a lot of gravy, so unless you are entertaining, you will have leftovers. It will keep in the refrigerator for up to 2 weeks.

*Makes 10 to 12 servings*

- 1/4 cup minced onion (see page 34)
- 4 tablespoons unsalted butter
- 1 tablespoon minced garlic (see page 34)
- 1 teaspoon red chili flakes
- 3/4 pound mild Pine Street Market or other high-quality ground pork country sausage
- 1 tablespoon kosher salt
- 1 1/3 cups all-purpose flour
- 5 cups Chicken Stock (page 36)
- 2 cups heavy cream
- 1/2 teaspoon ground nutmeg
- 4 dashes Tabasco sauce
- 2 teaspoons freshly ground black pepper
- 10 to 12 O.G. Buttermilk Biscuits (page 59)
- Clarified butter (see page 47)

Preheat a 4- to 6-quart saucepan over medium heat and begin cooking onion in butter. Once the onion is slightly amber, 2–3 minutes, add garlic and red chili flakes; continue to brown for 1–2 more minutes, and then add the sausage and salt. Stir, breaking up sausage with a wooden spoon, for another 5 minutes.

Gradually sprinkle in the flour while stirring. Once flour is incorporated, 1–2 minutes, slowly add stock while stirring. Increase heat to high and continue cooking until sauce comes to a boil and starts to thicken. Add cream and season with nutmeg, Tabasco, and pepper. Bring mixture up to a boil again while stirring. Remove from heat and cool slightly, about 5 minutes, to thicken.

To serve, cut open an O.G. Buttermilk Biscuit per person and griddle it with 1 tablespoon clarified butter. Smother some gravy all over the top and sit down for one of the most classic Southern breakfasts ever created.

# Blueberry-Basil Jam

*This is our house jam at the restaurant, and all of our biscuits and toast are served with it. The basil gives the blueberries a nice zing that makes you go "mmm." You could also substitute blackberries if that's your thing.*

*Makes about 12 cups*

- $1/4$ cup packed fresh basil leaves
- $1/4$ cup freshly squeezed orange juice
- 2 tablespoons freshly squeezed lemon juice
- 4 cups granulated sugar
- 5 pounds fresh blueberries (or substitute frozen)
- 1 tablespoon apple pectin

Combine basil with orange and lemon juice in a Vita-Prep or other high-speed blender. Blend 1–2 minutes on high until fully incorporated.

Add basil mixture to a large saucepan with the sugar and blueberries and bring to a boil, stirring frequently.

As berries are heating, purée mixture using an immersion blender (see page 23). You want to purée about half of the berries, leaving the other half intact. Cook until soft, 3–4 minutes.

Slowly add pectin while whisking vigorously and bring back to a boil for another 5 minutes. Turn off heat and cool. Store in the refrigerator for up to 2 weeks.

# Red Pepper Jelly

*Oh, Red Pepper Jelly, how I love you!
You tantalize the taste buds and hit all
the senses. The red pepper flakes and the
vinegar in this recipe balance the sugar,
producing sweet heat. This pepper jelly is
great on anything, an awesome counterpart
to our Pimento Cheese Spread (page 82),
and one of the key ingredients in our signature Pimento Cheese Omelet with Bacon
and Red Pepper Jelly (page 86). Make
some weekly to have on hand.*

*Makes 4 cups*

- 1 (28-ounce) can roasted diced red peppers, drained
- 2 teaspoons red pepper flakes
- 1 teaspoon kosher salt
- 3/4 cup apple cider vinegar
- 1 tablespoon unsalted butter
- 6 cups granulated sugar
- 2 teaspoons apple pectin

Place the red peppers in a food processor and pulse 4–5 times until peppers are
broken down and puréed.

Pour peppers into a medium saucepan,
add pepper flakes, salt, vinegar, butter, and
sugar, and bring to a full boil. Once mixture has reached a full boil, slowly mix in
pectin, whisking vigorously until slightly
thickened.

Return to a boil and cook for another
1–2 minutes, remove from heat, and cool.
This will keep for a about 2 weeks in the
refrigerator.

# Sriracha Butter

*We did a pop-up dinner one time that starred chicken and waffles. I was trying to come up with a sweet-and-spicy counterpart to the chicken, and that is how Sriracha Butter was born. People kind of freaked out about it and started asking for the recipe. I also like to use it to glaze roasted veggies, but that's for another cookbook.*

*Makes about ¹/₂ cup*

- 1 recipe Mason Jar Butter (page 71), 1 stick unsalted Banner Butter unsalted, or any other high-quality grass-fed butter

- 1 teaspoon Sriracha

- 1 tablespoon Little Bee honey or local honey

- 1 teaspoon orange zest

- 1 teaspoon Maldon sea salt

Add all ingredients to the bowl of a stand mixer equipped with the paddle attachment. Mix on medium speed for 2–3 minutes until ingredients are fully incorporated. Give it a taste, adjust additives as necessary, and place butter into a sealable container. The butter will keep for 7 days in the refrigerator or up to 1 month in the freezer.

# Mason Jar Butter

*When we first opened the restaurant, we made most of the butter we used in our recipes and to serve to our customers. As our business got bigger, making butter became too labor intensive, and we had to start purchasing high-quality butter for the restaurant. It's still fun to make butter, and this recipe is a great one to add to your repertoire.*

*Makes 3 ounces or almost 1 stick*

- 1 cup full-fat heavy cream
- 1 teaspoon full-fat sour cream
- 1 (16-ounce) regular Mason jar
- Cold water

Pour the cream and sour cream into the jar, filling it halfway full. Screw the lid on and shake the jar for 6–8 minutes. After the first 4 minutes, you'll have whipped cream. Keep shaking until a lump has formed inside, and shake an additional 30–60 seconds after that.

Remove the solids from the jar. The remaining liquid is buttermilk, which you can save for other recipes (like Buttermilk Whipped Cream (page 171)) or discard—just don't tell me you did.

Place the solids into a small bowl. Pour cold water over the butter and use your hands to squish it into a ball. Discard the water and repeat, rinsing 2 more times. At this point, you have butter. You can add in things like salt, honey, and herbs to create flavored butters, or serve as is.

Save that Mason jar and add to your drinking glass collection—it's the Southern thing to do.

# Honey-Lavender Butter

*We create a lot of specials and seasonal recipes at Buttermilk Kitchen. For Easter, my restaurant manager wanted to make a lavender-infused vodka for a specialty cocktail that called for fresh lavender. Surprisingly, I had never worked with fresh lavender, only dried. We called our flower lady and asked if she could get us some ("some" being the operative word) and were laughing when she showed up with ten plants! It turned out to be a great mistake, because I became obsessed with figuring out ways to use the abundance. Why had I not been working with lavender all this time? It's beautiful paired with honey and sea salt in this recipe. Try it as a garnish for your biscuits and gravy, use it to freshen up your bathroom, or just keep it around to have your house smelling fresh.*

*Makes about 1/2 cup*

- 1 recipe Mason Jar Butter (page 71), 1 stick unsalted Banner Butter, or any other high-quality grass-fed butter

- 2 stems fresh lavender*

- 1/8 cup Little Bee honey or local honey

- 1 teaspoon Maldon sea salt

Let butter come to room temperature, about 30 minutes, on the counter before starting this recipe. Do not rush or skip this step. You want the butter to be at the perfect temperature to ensure you can properly mix together all of the ingredients.

Remove fresh lavender leaves from the stem and finely mince on a cutting board.

Add all ingredients to the bowl of a stand mixer equipped with the paddle attachment. Mix on medium for 2–3 minutes until ingredients are fully incorporated. Give it a taste, adjust as needed, and place butter into a sealable container. The butter will keep for 7 days in the refrigerator or up to 1 month in the freezer.

*Fresh lavender can be located in the gardening section of a home department store or at your local farmers market.

# THE CHICKEN BISCUIT

When I first opened Buttermilk Kitchen, I never thought in a million years our chicken biscuits would become so popular. To tell you the truth, we only initially added them to a brunch special menu for variety. But variety was not the only thing those chicken biscuits accomplished. The chicken biscuit became the one dish Buttermilk is known for by nearly everyone. In fact, it became so unexpectedly popular that we originally could not keep up with the demand. The biscuits would sell out in the first few hours after opening each day. We had to ramp up production.

Here is our famous recipe for the Chicken Biscuit, and some variations. Enjoy!

# Chicken Biscuit

*Makes 2 biscuits*

- 2 (4-ounce) boneless and skinless chicken breasts
- 1 quart Sweet Tea Chicken Brine (page 35)
- 1 cup Fried Chicken Batter (page 37)
- 1 cup Fried Chicken Dredge (page 37)
- Canola oil
- 2 O.G. Buttermilk Biscuits (page 59)
- 2 tablespoons Red Pepper Jelly (page 68)
- Chopped parsley for garnish
- 4 to 5 House Pickles (page 38)

Place chicken in a large bowl, cover with brine, and refrigerate for at least 8 hours (but no longer than 12).

Remove chicken from brine, rinsing off any spices or herbs, and pat dry with paper towels. Place chicken in another bowl and pour the batter over it, turning to coat completely. Lift chicken out of bowl, letting excess batter drip off, and roll in the dredge, pressing down on both sides so the flour clings tightly to the brined chicken. Set on a baking sheet lined with wax paper while you prepare the oil.

Heat oil in a $4\frac{1}{2}$-quart saucepan or large cast iron skillet to 275 degrees. Use a deep-fry candy thermometer to monitor the temperature. Do not fill the pan more than halfway with oil.

Gently lay chicken into the oil and cook for 4 minutes on one side, adjusting heat as necessary to maintain 275 degrees. Flip chicken over and cook for an additional 5 minutes or until chicken registers 165 degrees.

Remove chicken from the pan and place on paper towels or a baking sheet lined with a cooling rack to drain and rest for at least 5 minutes.

Cut biscuits in half and slather bottom pieces with the jelly. Place fried chicken on top of jelly and close with top halves. Sprinkle with parsley and serve with pickles on the side.

## VARIATIONS

I've always wanted to open a chicken bis-cuit stand where all we serve is 5–6 rotating variations of chicken biscuits. Investors apply here! The combinations you can do with fried chicken and biscuits are endless. What follows are a couple we like to feature as specials.

### Hot Chicken Biscuit

Dip fried chicken, while still hot, into warmed Spiced Bacon Fat (page 48), coating all the way around. Place on a O.G. Buttermilk Biscuit (page 59) with Alabama Ranch (page 43) and House Pickles (page 38).

### Chicken Biscuit and Gravy

Split open a O.G. Buttermilk Biscuit (page 59) and put a piece of fried chicken on each side. Smother with about a cup of Sawmill Gravy (page 65) and garnish with chopped green onions. Get ready for a nap!

# Mole Chicken Biscuit

*My sous chef Christopher, known as Winnie, is from Mexico and makes an amazing mole sauce. It is so good that you can pretty much dip anything in it, including your shoe. We found ourselves most commonly dipping pieces of fried chicken into it. After a couple of tastes, the mole chicken biscuit was born.*

*Makes 1 biscuit*

1 O.G. Buttermilk Biscuit (page 59)

1 piece fried chicken (see page 76)

1 recipe Winnie's Mole Sauce (page 79)

1 tablespoon Mexican crema

3 to 4 pieces pickled red onion

Split open the biscuit and put 1 piece fried chicken on the bottom half of the biscuit. Reserve top piece of biscuit for later use—or just snack on it.

Pour $1/2$ cup warm mole sauce over chicken, drizzle with Mexican crema, and top with pickled red onions.

# WINNIE'S MOLE SAUCE

*Makes 1 quart*

- 2 tablespoons canola oil
- 2 cups minced onion (see page 34)
- 4 dried guajillo peppers, chopped
- 1/4 cup minced garlic (see page 34)
- 1/2 cup chili powder
- 4 tablespoons all-purpose flour
- 2 teaspoons ground cinnamon
- 2 teaspoons ground cumin
- 1 teaspoon dried Mexican oregano
- 5 cups Chicken Stock (page 36)
- 4 tablespoons smooth almond butter*
- 2 tablespoons tomato paste
- 2 tablespoons unsweetened cocoa powder
- 2 teaspoons Sriracha
- 3/4 cup brown sugar
- 2 teaspoons sea salt

Heat oil in a medium saucepan over medium-high heat. Add onion and guajillo peppers and sauté for 5 minutes, stirring occasionally, until soft and translucent. Add garlic and continue to sauté for 1–2 more minutes, stirring occasionally, until fragrant. Stir in chili powder, flour, cinnamon, cumin, and oregano until everything is evenly mixed.

Remove pan from heat. Pour in stock, and stir until combined.

In 2 small batches, transfer mixture to a blender and purée until smooth.

Pour puréed mixture into a clean saucepan over medium-high heat. Add almond butter, tomato paste, cocoa powder, Sriracha, brown sugar, and sea salt and whisk until combined. Continue cooking until the mixture reaches a simmer and the sauce has thickened.

Reduce heat to medium-low. Taste and season with more salt if needed. Store in an airtight container in the refrigerator for up to a week.

*Making your own almond butter is so satisfying. All you need is raw almonds, a pinch of sea salt, and a food processor. If buying, get a good brand, such as Barney.

# PIMENTO CHEESE

We are definitely known for our pimento cheese at Buttermilk Kitchen; we go through about sixty pounds a week. You will find it in several of our recipes, like Pimento Cheese Omelet with Bacon and Red Pepper Jelly (page 86), Pimento Cheese Grits (page 84), or slathered on toast in our Fried Pickled Green Tomato Melt (page 89). At the first restaurant I owned, the Hungry Peach, we were known for our pimento cheese. I knew when I opened Buttermilk Kitchen that we would also need a good version, and I like to think we have the best in town.

# Pimento Cheese Spread

*Pimento cheese is an extremely versatile ingredient, so I encourage you to keep a batch on hand at all times. If you want to be a boss, make your own roasted red peppers by charring them over an open flame and dicing them into small pieces. If not, a store-bought brand like Roland's pimentos work just fine. I suggest mixing this recipe with your hands, because massaging the pimento cheese is a crucial step in achieving the right consistency. If you do not have time to make your own mayonnaise, substitute Duke's brand if you can.*

*Serves 10 to 12 or makes 4 cups*

 1 pound sharp cheddar cheese, grated

 1 cup Mayonnaise (page 45)

 1/2 cup small diced fire-roasted red peppers (pimentos), drained

 2 teaspoons Sriracha

 2 teaspoons minced onion (see page 34)

 1/2 teaspoon kosher salt

 1 teaspoon freshly ground black pepper

Place all ingredients in a medium-size mixing bowl. Combine, using your hands, massaging the ingredients until thoroughly combined. Taste for seasoning and adjust if needed.

Transfer pimento cheese to an airtight container and store in the refrigerator for up to 1 week.

## VARIATIONS

Who says you have to stick to just regular pimento cheese? There are many different ways to jazz it up. Give one of these options a try!

### Mexican Cheese
Using the same amounts, swap out the pimentos with roasted poblanos, and use Chihuahua Mexican cheese in place of the cheddar.

### Ramp Cheese
There is a small period of time in the spring when ramps (wild leeks) are in season. Ramps have a delicious, garlicky flavor that pairs nicely with the sharp cheddar. Using the same amount, swap out pimentos with the ramps.

**Cacio e Pepe Pimento Cheese**
This is a twist on the classic Italian dish Cacio e Pepe. Substitute freshly grated Parmesan cheese for the cheddar cheese, remove the salt and Sriracha, and double the amount of black pepper.

# Pimento Cheese Snack

*This is one of the appetizers served at the restaurant. It is a great spread for entertaining; try it at your next dinner party. You can arrange this any way you like, but this is how we do it. Try dipping your toast in Classic French Toast batter (page 95) before grilling for a breakfast spin.*

*Serves 4 to 6*

> 1 cup Pimento Cheese Spread
> (page 82)
>
> Handful of House Pickles
> (page 38)
>
> 1/4 cup Red Pepper Jelly
> (page 68)
>
> 2 pieces thick-sliced white bread, grilled in butter and cut into 4 pieces each
>
> 1 recipe Biscuit Crackers
> (page 174)
>
> Paprika for garnish

Place the pimento cheese in the center of a large plate or platter. Nestle the pickles next to the cheese. Put the jelly in a 4-ounce wide-mouth Mason jar and set it by the cheese and pickles. Arrange toast and Biscuit Crackers around the outside edges and garnish the cheese with a sprinkle of paprika.

# Pimento Cheese Butter

*Making this butter is a great way to utilize a small amount of leftover pimento cheese. It is delicious on top of a steak, on Reggae Grits (page 143), or over a baked potato.*

*Makes about 1 cup*

- 1/2 pound (2 sticks) unsalted Banner Butter, or any other high-quality, grass-fed butter

- 3 tablespoons Pimento Cheese Spread (page 82)

- 2 teaspoons sea salt

Set the butter on the counter for about 30 minutes before starting this recipe. Don't rush or skip this step. You want the butter to be at the perfect temperature to ensure you can properly mix together all of the ingredients.

Add the butter, pimento cheese, and salt to the mixing bowl of a stand mixer equipped with a paddle attachment. Mix on medium for 2–3 minutes until ingredients are fully incorporated. Give it a taste, adjust to taste if needed, and put butter into a sealable container. It should last at least 7 days in the refrigerator or up to 1 month in the freezer.

# Pimento Cheese Grits

*We serve these grits with our iconic Chicken Biscuits (page 76). They are also great on their own or mixed with proteins or sautéed vegetables. I like to fold in chopped, cooked bacon or diced sausage links right as the grits come off the stove.*

*Serves 8 to 10*

- 2 cups prepared Reggae Grits (page 143)

- 1/4 teaspoon kosher salt

- 1/2 cup Pimento Cheese Spread (page 82)

Put grits, salt, and pimento cheese in a 4 1/2-quart saucepan over low heat. Whisk ingredients until flavors are combined and cheese is melted, about 5 minutes.

# Pimento Cheese Omelet with Bacon and Red Pepper Jelly

*This is one of our signature dishes at the restaurant. We pair the pimento cheese with smoky bacon from Benton's Country Hams in Tennessee. The bacon is so smoky that even the packing invoice shows up saturated in bacon grease. We serve this omelet with one of our signature O.G. Buttermilk Biscuits (page 59) and a side of Sautéed Kale (page 138). I like to make a sandwich, layering the omelet inside the biscuit. It's the best bacon, egg, and cheese you will ever have!*

*Makes 1 omelet*

> 2 slices thick-cut Benton's bacon or other high-quality bacon, cut into $1/2$-inch pieces
>
> 3 eggs
>
> 1 tablespoon unsalted butter
>
> Pinch of kosher salt
>
> 2 tablespoons Pimento Cheese Spread (page 82)
>
> 1 tablespoon Red Pepper Jelly (page 68)

Slowly cook bacon in a large cast iron skillet over medium-low heat for about 20 minutes. Cooking slowly over a low heat will render out as much fat as possible. Bacon should still be pliable and not crispy. Once bacon is done, remove from skillet using a slotted spoon and let drain on paper towels.

Crack the eggs into a small mixing bowl and lightly beat using a fork or small whisk.

Preheat an 8-inch nonstick skillet over medium heat for about 30 seconds. Add butter to pan. The butter should start to sizzle but not brown. If butter starts to brown, your pan is too hot and you will need to start over. If the butter barely melts, your pan is too cold.

Add eggs to the skillet and do not stir for 30 seconds to 1 minute, allowing eggs to set. Add salt. Once the eggs start to set, gently start dragging a silicone spatula all the way through the omelet from all sides, forming large curds; this ensures that the raw parts of the eggs get cooked. You want to work quickly so the bottom of your omelet does not burn or brown. Once the eggs are mostly set and curds are formed, flip your omelet over. If you haven't achieved flipping status quite yet, you can always let the omelet finish cooking in a preheated 350 degree oven for 3–4 minutes.

As soon as the omelet is done, spread pimento cheese across the center, then add bacon, and top with pepper jelly. Using your spatula, lift under omelet, fold in half, and slide onto a plate.

# Fried Pickled Green Tomato Melt

*Fried green tomatoes are big in the South; you don't have to watch the movie to know that. However, I always find them lacking in flavor. Instead of using plain green tomatoes, we give them a bath in our Pickling Brine (page 40) before we batter and fry them.*

*Makes 1 sandwich*

- 1/2 cup Pimento Cheese Spread (page 82)

- 2 (1/2-inch-thick) slices multigrain or whole-wheat bread

- 4 slices Fried Pickled Green Tomatoes (page 150)

Before making this sandwich, let the pimento cheese come to room temperature (about 30 minutes) so it is easy to spread on the bread.

Toast the bread in a toaster or in a 350-degree oven for about 5 minutes. Divide the pimento cheese between the 2 pieces of bread and evenly spread.

Place tomatoes in a single layer on top of pimento cheese on 1 slice of bread. Close sandwich with second piece of bread and cut in half diagonally.

VARIATION  For an extra flavor kick, add 2 slices of cooked bacon on top of the green tomatoes.

# FROM THE GRIDDLE

We serve up griddle classics you see on most American tables, like our O.G. Buttermilk Pancakes (page 92), Classic French Toast (page 95), and sausage and bacon. The grill cook has a very important job at Buttermilk Kitchen, to say the least.

# O.G. Buttermilk Pancakes

*People love our pancakes and always ask us how we get them so fluffy. We make our batter fresh each morning and use great ingredients. It's important to separate the wet ingredients from the dry ones when making this batter. You want to fully incorporate the ingredients, but not overmix the batter.*

*Makes about 8 large pancakes*

- 1 stick European-style unsalted butter, plus extra
- 2 1/4 cups Banner Butter buttermilk or other high-quality, full-fat buttermilk
- 1/4 cup whole milk
- 1/2 tablespoon full-fat sour cream
- 2 large eggs
- 2 cups all-purpose flour
- 1/4 cup granulated sugar
- 3 tablespoons baking powder
- 1 teaspoon kosher salt
- Sweet Toppings, of choice (see pages 101–107)

Melt butter in microwave and set aside to cool.

Add the buttermilk, whole milk, sour cream, and eggs to the bowl of a stand mixer fitted with the whisk attachment. Mix on medium speed until ingredients are incorporated, about 2 minutes.

Using a whisk, mix together the flour, sugar, baking powder, and salt in a medium mixing bowl. Reduce mixer speed to low, add half of the dry ingredients to the wet ingredients, and mix for about 30 seconds. Add the remaining dry ingredients and mix until just incorporated. Scrape down the sides of the bowl with a silicone spatula.

Add melted butter and mix for 20 more seconds or until butter is just mixed into the batter. Let rest while you prepare the griddle.

Preheat a griddle or large nonstick sauté pan over medium-low heat and brush with butter. Using a 4-ounce ice cream scoop, scoop batter onto hot griddle and cook until bubbly on top and golden on the bottom, about 4 minutes. Flip and cook until golden on the other side, about 2 more minutes.

# Classic French Toast

*I can still remember the first time I tasted French toast. I was in love. Buttery toast dipped in egg batter and griddled to per-fection—what could be better? There is nothing fancy about our French toast, and it's perhaps the simplest menu item we have. People seem to really appreciate its simplicity, and it's been a staple dish since opening.*

*Makes about 4 servings*

6 eggs

1 cup full-fat heavy cream

1 cup whole milk

1 tablespoon real maple syrup

1/2 tablespoon freshly ground nutmeg

1/2 tablespoon vanilla extract

1 teaspoon kosher salt

1 to 2 tablespoons unsalted butter

4 (1-inch-thick) slices Southern white or challah bread

Confectioners' sugar

Sweet Toppings, of choice (see pages 101–107)

Whisk the eggs together in a medium mixing bowl. Add the cream, milk, maple syrup, nutmeg, vanilla extract, and salt. Whisk everything together and set aside.

Preheat a griddle or large nonstick sauté pan over medium-low heat and brush with butter.

Gently dip each slice of bread into the egg batter, coating both sides, and place on a wire rack to allow excess batter to drip off.

Add battered bread to the griddle and cook for 2–3 minutes on each side until golden brown. If bread starts to turn too dark and is still raw in the center, you can finish cooking it in a 350 degree oven, or use a steak weight (see page 25) to weigh down the bread, cooking it faster.

Top with a sprinkle of confectioners' sugar and any Sweet Topping.

# Cobbler Biscuit French Toast

*This is a fun spin on traditional French toast. If you can't find mascarpone cheese, substitute a high-quality cream cheese instead.*

*Makes 1 serving*

- 1 tablespoon unsalted butter
- 1 O.G. Buttermilk Biscuit (page 59)
- 1 cup Classic French Toast batter (page 95)
- $1/2$ cup Strawberry Compote (page 104) or Blueberry Compote (page 107), warmed
- Mascarpone Frosting
- 1 tablespoon Pie Crumb (page 165)

Preheat a griddle or large nonstick sauté pan over medium-low heat and brush with butter. Slice biscuit in half horizontally. Gently dip each biscuit half into batter, coating both sides, and place on a wire rack to allow excess batter to drip off. Place biscuit halves on the griddle and cook 2–3 minutes per side until golden brown.

Place 1 biscuit half in a serving bowl and pour warm compote over top. Close with remaining biscuit half and top with Mascarpone Frosting and pie crumbs.

## MASCARPONE FROSTING

*Makes about 2 cups*

- 2 tablespoons European-style unsalted butter, softened
- 4 ounces ($1/4$ pound) mascarpone cheese
- $1/2$ teaspoon vanilla extract
- $1^{1}/2$ cups confectioners' sugar

For the Mascarpone Frosting, beat the butter and mascarpone together using an electric mixer with paddle attachment until completely smooth, about 3 minutes on medium speed. Use a rubber spatula to scrape down the sides of the mixing bowl to ensure that the mixture is mixed evenly. Beat in the vanilla, and with the mixer running on low speed, slowly add in confectioners' sugar until fully incorporated.

# Nashville Hot Griddled Cornbread with Honey

*Makes 1 serving*

- 1 tablespoon unsalted butter
- 1 mini Cornbread loaf (page 156)
- 2 tablespoons Spiced Bacon Fat (page 48), warmed
- 1 tablespoon honey
- Minced chives

Preheat a cast iron skillet over medium heat and brush with butter. Cut cornbread loaf in half vertically. Place cornbread halves in skillet and lightly press down using a steak weight (see page 25). Cook for 1–2 minutes, flip over, and cook another 1–2 minutes until golden brown. Brush tops with bacon fat.

Place griddled cornbread on a plate and garnish with honey and chives.

# Johnny Cakes with Liquid Gold

*This is a special recipe using our Cornbread batter (page 156) and Little Bee's spun honey, or "liquid gold," as I like to call it. Spun honey is achieved by whipping crystalized honey with normal honey and then breaking up the larger crystals, which results in a smooth, spreadable texture.*

*Makes 8 cakes*

- 2 tablespoons unsalted butter or bacon fat (see page 48)

- 1 cup prepared Cornbread batter (page 156)

- Orange zest

- 1 to 2 tablespoons spun honey

- Banner Butter, or other high-quality, grass-fed butter for serving (optional)

Preheat a cast iron skillet over medium-low heat and brush with butter or bacon fat.

Scoop batter into the skillet in 8 (2-tablespoon) portions. Cook until bubbly on top and golden on the bottom, about 4 minutes. Flip and cook until golden on the on the other side, 1–2 more minutes, until brown and crisp.

Remove from skillet and serve immediately with orange zest, spun honey, and butter, if using.

# SWEET TOPPINGS

Pancakes and French toast are great plain, but just like biscuits, they are a perfect canvas for many toppings. Pancakes are like sponges and will soak up any flavor headed their way.

# Caramelized Banana

*Caramelized bananas are fun to make, and are an easy way to impress your friends. They are a signature garnish for our Caramelized-Banana Oatmeal (page 126), and my favorite way to top pancakes. You will need a kitchen torch for these. You could also use your broiler, but you won't get the same crust.*

*Makes 1 to 2 servings*

> 1 organic banana
>
> 4 teaspoons raw sugar

With banana still in its peel, slice in half horizontally. Evenly spread 2 teaspoons raw sugar over each half of banana. Using a crème brûlée torch, brûlée sugar on banana halves, moving the flame back in forth for about 30 seconds until a dark brown crust has formed. Remove banana from peel before serving.

# Rye Whiskey Maple Syrup

*We love our friends over at American Spirit Whiskey, the local distillery in Atlanta. We use their rye whiskey in this recipe, as it pairs wonderfully with the maple syrup.*

*Makes 1 cup*

> 2 tablespoons ASW Resurgens Rye, or your favorite rye whiskey
>
> 1 cup real maple syrup

In a small saucepan, whisk whiskey and syrup together over low heat. Bring mixture to a simmer and cook for about 5 minutes, just until the flavor infuses.

Remove from heat and serve immediately. If not using right away, cool, cover, and refrigerate for 3–5 days.

# Vanilla Whipped Cream

*Whipped cream is one of the simplest things to make, yet one of the things people always seem to buy. Make your own and you will taste the difference. You will need an iSi whipper (see page 25) or a stand mixer fitted with a whisk attachment.*

*Makes 2 cups*

   1 cup full-fat heavy cream

   1 tablespoon confectioners' sugar

   1/2 teaspoon vanilla extract

Mix together ingredients in a small mixing bowl and then pour into a 16-ounce iSi whipping siphon. Secure lid and add 2 No.2 cartridges. Shake vigorously before dispensing. If using a stand mixer, add all ingredients to bowl of mixer and mix on low, using whisk attachment, for 1–2 minutes until cream starts to stiffen. Increase speed to medium and continue to mix for another 1–2 minutes until cream is whipped.

# Strawberry Compote

*Everyone loves a good strawberry jam. Use strawberries when in peak season. If you prefer a sweeter jam, double the amount of sugar.*

*Makes 2 cups*

   1 1/2 pounds strawberries, hulled, washed, and quartered

   1/4 cup freshly squeezed orange juice

   1/4 cup granulated sugar

Add all ingredients to a medium saucepan and cook over medium heat, stirring frequently until sauce slightly thickens, about 15 minutes.

Remove from heat and pour on top of pancakes or French toast, or cool and store in an airtight container in the refrigerator for up to 2 weeks.

# Spiced Citrus Compote

*This is an awesome pancake topping when citrus is in season. This would also pair nicely with an O.G. Buttermilk Biscuit (page 59). I use Cara Cara and blood oranges when they are in season, but if you can't find them, you can substitute regular oranges.*

*Makes 2 cups*

- 1 tablespoon Cara Cara orange zest
- 1/4 cup freshly squeezed grapefruit juice
- 1/4 cup water
- 1/2 cup granulated sugar
- 1/2 teaspoon whole cloves
- 1/2 teaspoon ground allspice
- 1/2 teaspoon ground cinnamon
- 1/8 cup dried cherries
- 1 cup blood orange segments (about 4 oranges)
- 2 cups Cara Cara segments (about 3 oranges)

Combine zest, grapefruit juice, water, sugar, cloves, allspice, and cinnamon in a 4- to 6-quart saucepan and bring to a boil while stirring. Reduce mixture to a simmer and cook, stirring continuously, until sugar is completely dissolved and mixture thickens, about 10 minutes. It should be the consistency of maple syrup.

Strain mixture through a chinois or fine-mesh strainer and set aside.

Combine cherries, blood orange, and Cara Cara segments together in a large plastic container or mixing bowl. Pour strained mixture over segments and stir together.

# Blueberry Compote

*This is a great accompaniment to French toast or pancakes. We make this in late summer when blueberries are at their peak. You could also substitute blackberries.*

*Makes 2 cups*

- 4 cups blueberries, fresh or frozen
- 1/2 cup granulated sugar
- 1 1/2 teaspoons lemon juice
- 1 tablespoon cornstarch

Place blueberries, sugar, and lemon juice in a medium saucepan and cook over medium heat, stirring until sauce slightly thickens, about 5 minutes.

Remove excess liquid from the saucepan and pour into a small mixing bowl with the cornstarch. Whisk together until cornstarch is smooth then pour back into the saucepan with blueberries.

Bring mixture to a full boil and cook for 3–5 minutes, stirring frequently. Remove from heat and serve immediately, or cool and store in an airtight container in the refrigerator for up to 2 weeks.

# CLASSICS

You will find the recipes in this chapter on our menu all year long. They define Buttermilk Kitchen in some way or another, and are the dishes that I couldn't imagine not having for breakfast or brunch. They are classics.

# EGGS YOUR WAY

There is nothing more classic than two eggs cooked the way you want them. We do have a couple stipulations when it comes to cooking eggs; here is the way you can get them.

# Poached

*There is nothing more classic than two perfectly poached eggs. If you can master poached eggs, you are a boss in my book. I love when people order their eggs this style; I always know they are my type of people.*

*Makes 1 serving*

- 4 to 6 cups water
- 2 tablespoons white or cider vinegar
- 2 whole eggs
- Pinch of Maldon sea salt

In a 4- to 6-quart saucepan, combine water and vinegar and bring to a boil over high heat.

As soon as the water comes to a boil, reduce heat to medium high and, using a whisk, stir water 2–3 times to create a whirlpool. Crack each egg into a small bowl then release into the water and let it do its magic. The vinegar in the water will help the egg whites coagulate around the yolk, and after 1–2 minutes of cooking, it will float to the surface. Use a slotted spoon to lift eggs out of the water and gently poke your finger in the middle to test for doneness. The whites should be completely set and the middle should be jiggly. Place eggs back in the water if you like the yolks to cook longer.

When eggs are to your liking, drain on paper towels, place in a small serving bowl, and sprinkle with sea salt.

# Fried

*Fried eggs mean a lot of different things to a lot of different people. Technically, fried eggs are any egg cooked in a pan. But when you come to Buttermilk and order a fried egg, we are going to fry them in a pan, break the yolks, and cook them all the way through.*

*Makes 1 serving*

> 1 teaspoon clarified butter (see page 47)
>
> 1 or 2 whole eggs
>
> Pinch of kosher salt

Heat an 8-inch nonstick skillet over medium heat. Add clarified butter and swirl to coat bottom of skillet.

Crack egg(s) into skillet and cook for about 10 seconds or until whites start to set; season with salt. Using a silicone spatula, break yolks completely and continue to cook for another 30 seconds until whites have completely set. Using your spatula, release egg from around sides of pan to prevent it from sticking. Flip eggs over by tilting nose of pan toward the flame and flipping back quickly using wrist action, or carefully flip using the spatula. Let eggs cook for about 1–2 minutes then slide onto a plate and serve.

If you haven't mastered the egg flip yet, you can finish your eggs in a 350-degree oven for 1–2 minutes. If you want to learn, practicing with a piece of bread is a great way to master the wrist action.

# Over-Easy (Runny Yolk)

*The runny yolks from over-easy eggs are delicious over grits and potatoes.*

*Makes 1 serving*

1 teaspoon clarified butter (see page 47)

1 or 2 whole eggs

Pinch of kosher salt

Heat an 8-inch nonstick skillet over medium heat. Add clarified butter and swirl to coat bottom of skillet.

Crack egg(s) into pan and cook for about 1 minute or until whites have set. Season with salt. Using a silicone spatula, release eggs around sides of pan to prevent from sticking.

Flip eggs over by tilting nose of pan toward the flame and flipping back quickly using wrist action, or carefully flip using the spatula. Let eggs cook for about 10 more seconds then slide onto a plate and serve.

# Over-Medium (Slightly Runny Yolk)

*Over-medium eggs are very similar to over-easy eggs, but cooked slightly longer and the yolks are slightly oozy.*

*Makes 1 serving*

> 1 teaspoon clarified butter (see page 47)
>
> 1 or 2 whole eggs
>
> Pinch of kosher salt

Heat an 8-inch nonstick skillet over medium heat. Add clarified butter and swirl to coat bottom of skillet.

Crack egg(s) into pan and cook for about 1 minute or until whites have set. Season with salt. Using a silicone spatula, release eggs around sides of pan to prevent from sticking.

Flip eggs over by tilting nose of pan toward the flame and flipping back quickly using wrist action, or carefully flip using the spatula. Let eggs cook for about 1 minute or until yolks are slightly firm to the touch then slide onto a plate and serve.

# Sunny-Side-Up

*What is more sexy than perfectly cooked, bright, sunny eggs? Even people eating sunny eggs look sexy. People that order their eggs sunny should get a special pat on the back.*

*Makes 1 serving*

    1 teaspoon clarified butter (see page 47)

    1 or 2 whole eggs

    Pinch of kosher salt

Heat an 8-inch nonstick skillet over medium heat. Add clarified butter and swirl to coat bottom of skillet.

Crack egg(s) into pan and cook for about 1 minute or until whites have set. Season with salt. Using a silicone spatula, drag uncooked parts of egg whites toward outer edge of pan, being careful not to break the yolk.

Turn heat down to low and continue to cook for another minute. If the white has still not set all the way, you can finish the egg in a 350-degree oven for 30 seconds–1 minute, but make sure you are using an ovenproof pan. Slide onto a plate and serve.

# Scrambled

*Perfectly scrambled eggs are an art form in themselves. When done right, they are creamy and only need salt. I cringe when people order scramble eggs hard; to me it's like ordering a steak well done.*

*Makes 1 serving*

> 1 tablespoon clarified butter (see page 47)
>
> 1 or 2 whole eggs
>
> Pinch of kosher salt

Heat an 8-inch nonstick skillet over high heat. When skillet is rippling hot and just about to smoke, remove from heat, add clarified butter, and swirl to coat bottom of skillet.

Crack egg(s) into skillet and immediately stir with a silicone spatula, breaking the yolks and mixing until whites and yolks are completely blended. While stirring, return skillet to heat, then take back off again. Repeat this in ten-second intervals until eggs start to set. Season with salt and keep stirring until eggs are broken up and slightly set. Take off heat just before you think they are done; the eggs will continue to cook in the skillet. Slide onto a plate and serve.

# Market Scramble

*We always have a market scramble on the menu highlighting the season's best vegetables. You can get as creative as you want here with proteins, vegetables, and cheese. I've included some of our most popular seasonal vegetables that are amazing in scrambles.*

*Makes 1 to 2 servings*

  3 whole eggs

  1 tablespoon clarified butter (see page 47)

  $1/2$ cup seasonal vegetables, of choice (see pages 117–118)

  $1/4$ cup grated cheese, preferably local and easy melting (Gouda, mozzarella, or Asiago)

  Pinch of kosher salt

Crack eggs into a small mixing bowl, and using a fork, break up the eggs and beat until eggs are completely liquid.

Preheat a 9-inch nonstick skillet over medium heat for about 30 seconds; add butter. The butter should start to sizzle but not brown.

Add prepared vegetables to skillet and cook until warmed through, about 1 minute. Add eggs, and using a silicone spatula, vigorously stir the eggs and vegetables to break up the egg curds. Once eggs have almost completely set, 2–3 minutes, add cheese and let melt, about 30 seconds. Season with salt and serve immediately.

# SUMMERTIME TOMATO CONFIT

*This is a great recipe when tomatoes are at their peak in the summer. It is excellent in a scramble or served as a side.*

*Makes 4 to 5 cups*

6 pounds local cherry tomatoes

$1^1/2$ cups blended oil

2 tablespoons kosher salt

1 tablespoon ground black pepper

$1/2$ cup minced garlic (see page 34)

1 bunch fresh thyme

Preheat oven to 300 degrees.

Spread the tomatoes in a baking dish. Add oil, salt, pepper, and garlic; toss gently to coat. Add bunch of thyme, tucking into tomato mixture.

Bake for $1^1/2$–2 hours until tomatoes are wilted but not all have burst. Cool tomatoes to room temperature; discard thyme and drain tomatoes, saving tomato oil for another use.

# FALL ROASTED PUMPKIN

*This recipe calls for a pie pumpkin, which is easily found at grocery stores and markets in the fall. You could substitute butternut squash, as well.*

*Makes about 1 cup*

1 pie pumpkin

2 tablespoons high-quality olive oil

Pinch of red pepper flakes

1 teaspoon kosher salt

Preheat oven to 375 degrees.

Cut the top and bottom end off of pumpkin using a sharp knife. Using a peeler, remove outer layer of skin. Cut peeled pumpkin in half and remove seeds and inner flesh. Dice pumpkin into $1/2$-inch cubes and place in a medium mixing bowl.

Season pumpkin with oil, pepper flakes, and salt to taste. Lay out on sheet pan in an even layer. Roast for 10 minutes. Pumpkin should be tender but slightly firm to the touch. Set aside to cool.

# ANYTIME BALSAMIC MUSHROOMS

*You find mushrooms predominantly in the fall, but they are available all year. They are great in a scramble or slathered on buttered toast.*

*Makes about 2 cups*

- 1 tablespoon olive oil
- 1-pound mix of mushrooms (such as oyster, chanterelles, baby bellas)
- 4 tablespoons ($1/2$ stick) unsalted butter
- 1 tablespoon minced garlic (see page 34)
- 1 white onion, thinly sliced
- 1 teaspoon salt
- 1 teaspoon black pepper
- $1/4$ cup balsamic vinegar

Heat oil over medium heat in a large skillet or cast iron pan. Add mushrooms and cook until light brown, about 5 minutes. Add butter, garlic, onion, salt, and pepper and cook for another 2–3 minutes. Pour in balsamic vinegar and simmer until liquid is almost evaporated, about 15 minutes. Set aside to cool then taste for seasoning.

# CREAMED SPRING ONIONS

*Spring onions are delicate and delicious. They are very young onions harvested before the bulb gets large, yielding a mild and sweet flavor.*

*Makes about 2 cups*

- 2 tablespoons unsalted butter
- $1/8$ cup honey
- 4 cups sliced spring onions (bulb and green tops)
- $1/2$ cup Chicken Stock (page 36) or vegetable stock
- Salt, to taste
- Pepper, to taste
- 1 teaspoon ground nutmeg
- 1 cup heavy whipping cream

In a 4- to 6-quart saucepan, melt butter; stir in honey until blended. Add onions, stock, salt, pepper, and nutmeg. Bring to a boil. Reduce heat; simmer, covered, 15 minutes or until onions are tender.

Cook, uncovered, over medium-high heat another 15–20 minutes or until liquid is almost evaporated, stirring occasionally. Stir in cream and cook 3–5 minutes longer or until sauce is thickened. Let cool.

# Ray's Waffle Burger

This is a riff on my dad's favorite breakfast.

Growing up, I had many opportunities to indulge in home-cooked meals inspired by secret recipes handed down from my Italian grandmother (Nonna), my dad's mother. I often tagged along in the kitchen as my dad prepared his famous pastas, mouth-watering steaks, and delicious tomato platters. Even before organic was hip, my dad was growing fresh basil and mint to pair with entrées and iced teas.

When I was still very young, the genesis of the "hamburger on a waffle" transpired. One morning, my dad awoke looking forward to his traditional breakfast of bacon and waffles, only to discover that all of the bacon had mysteriously vanished from the refrigerator. While pondering the idea of disrupting his relaxing morning at home and embarking on a dreaded trip to the grocery store, he remembered that he had just purchased a lean beef patty. Typically, he would marinate the burger with Worcestershire sauce, sea salt, and ground black pepper. Then he would heat the grill to high, sear the patty to medium-rare perfection, and drop it onto a bun. Armed with a bit of ingenuity, he instead paired the juicy hamburger with a waffle and finished it off with a dash of syrup. Not only was he pleased with this new breakfast invention, it became his annual Father's Day request.

Years later, when I opened Buttermilk Kitchen, it only seemed fitting to reserve a special place on the menu for Dad's cherished breakfast creation. He was my hero and a big reason I am where I am today in my cooking career. In his honor, we serve this dish at brunch and donate one dollar from each dish sold to local pet therapy organizations, which aided and comforted him while he was sick. He is missed.

## Makes 1 burger

- 4 ounces mild Pine Street Market or other high-quality ground pork country sausage

- 4 ounces ground Painted Hills or other high-quality, grass-fed beef

- 1 ounce grated pepper jack cheese

- 1 to 2 tablespoons Coffee Rub (page 50)

- 1/2 cup (or more, depending on your waffle maker) O.G. Buttermilk Pancake batter (page 92)

- 2 tablespoons Maple Aioli (page 46)

- 2 slices Hormel sugar-cured cooked bacon

Mix sausage and beef together in a mixing bowl until thoroughly combined. Divide mixture in half, roll into 2 balls, and place on a flat surface or cutting board. Using your hands, gently shape and press the balls into rectangular patties about the size of an index card and about 3/4 inch thick. Using your hands, roll the grated cheese into a ball, place in the center of 1 of the patties, and cover with the other patty. Crimp edges with your fingers to ensure that the patties are sealed together and the cheese does not ooze out while grilling.

Preheat grill or cast iron skillet to medium-high heat.

On a plate or small dish, rub burger patty all over with Coffee Rub and place on grill. Using a steak weight, press burger and cook for 4–5 minutes. Remove weight, flip burger, replace weight, and cook for another 4–5 minutes or until internal temperature registers 155 degrees. Place burger on a plate or tray fitted with a wire rack and let rest while you prepare the waffle.

Preheat a waffle iron according to manufacturer's instructions.

Spray waffle iron with nonstick cooking spray. Pour batter onto hot waffle iron. Cook until golden brown. Cut waffle in half horizontally and then cut off the ends of each half.

Slather the waffle pieces with Maple Aioli and place cooked burger on bottom half. Top with bacon slices and close with other waffle half. Enjoy, and then take a nap!

*Note* We use a round waffle maker. You can use a different shape, but you may have to cut the waffle to fit the shape of the burger patty. It's also best to have a steak weight when cooking the burger to achieve a good sear, locking in all those flavors. If you do not have a steak weight, you can easily make one by wrapping a brick in aluminum foil.

# B.E.L.T. (Bacon. Egg. Lettuce. Tomato.)

*This sandwich is EVERYTHING and has been on the menu since we opened. The red tomatoes balance the acidity from the Pickled Green Tomatoes and Lemon Mayonnaise, and the bacon and egg top it off for the ultimate brunch.*

*Makes 1 sandwich*

- 2 slices multigrain or bread of choice, lightly toasted

- 1 tablespoon Lemon Mayonnaise (page 46)

- Handful of baby spinach

- Lemon oil

- 2 to 3 slices red tomato

- 2 to 3 slices Pickled Green Tomatoes (page 38)

- 2 slices Hormel sugar-cured cooked bacon

- 1 egg Over-Medium (Slightly Runny Yolk) (page 113)

Spread both sides of toast with Lemon Mayonnaise.

In a small mixing bowl, toss spinach in lemon oil and place on bottom piece of toast. Add red and green tomatoes. Tear pieces of cooked bacon in half and place on top of tomatoes. Top with egg and the other piece of toast. Now take a big bite—you're welcome!

# Local Grit Bowl

*This is a complete breakfast for me—you get everything you need. If you don't like grits, substitute oats.*

*Makes 1 serving*

*Garlic Spinach*

    1 tablespoon clarified butter (see page 47)

    1 teaspoon minced garlic (see page 34)

    Pinch of red pepper flakes

    $1/2$ teaspoon salt

    2 cups fresh baby spinach

*Charred Lemon*

    1 teaspoon coconut oil

    $1/2$ lemon

    1 tablespoon brown sugar

*Grits*

    1 cup cooked Reggae Grits (page 143)

    3 links grilled chicken sausage, diced into $1/2$-inch pieces

    1 cup prepared Garlic Spinach

    2 eggs cooked to choice (see pages 111–116)

    1 Charred Lemon

*Garlic Spinach* Heat a cast iron skillet over medium-high heat. Add clarified butter and minced garlic and sauté for about 30 seconds. Add red pepper flakes and salt and cook for another 30 seconds. Add spinach and cook just until spinach starts to wilt, using tongs to stir. Remove pan from heat.

*Charred Lemon* Add a drizzle of coconut oil to a small skillet over medium heat. Dip the cut side of the lemon in the brown sugar and place the lemon, cut side down, in the skillet to cook for 6–8 minutes. The cut side should be browned with a sugar crust when taken off the heat. Let the lemon cool.

*Grits* Place the grits in the bottom of a soup or serving bowl. Top with sausage, Garlic Spinach, and eggs. Garnish with lemon.

**VARIATIONS** Grit bowls are a fun way to make your own creations. You can try adding more savory ingredients for a quick dinner. Try adding blue or cheddar cheese to your grits in the final cooking stage. Replace sausage with diced bacon, or for the vegetarians out there, top with roasted eggplant, Sautéed Kale (page 138), or Summertime Tomato Confit (page 117).

# Caramelized-Banana Oatmeal

*This is one of my favorite items on the menu. I absolutely love cooked bananas, and here they lend the perfect amount of sweetness to the oatmeal. We use Anson Mills (https://ansonmills.com/products) stone-cut oats, as they have a wonderful coarse texture. You can buy them on the company website, and even though you could substitute regular oats here, I highly suggest you don't.*

*Makes 1 serving*

- 1/2 cup Anson Mills stone-cut oats
- 1/2 teaspoon kosher salt
- 1 1/2 cups water
- 1/4 cup diced banana
- 1 half Caramelized Banana (page 102) for serving
- 1 to 2 tablespoons Vanilla Whipped Cream (page 104)
- Dash of cinnamon, optional

Place the oats and salt in a 4- to 6-quart saucepan and pour the water over them. Stir once. Allow the oats to settle for 1 minute, tilt the pan, and skim off and discard the hulls of the oats with a fine-mesh strainer.

Set the saucepan over low heat. Partially cover and bring the oats to a simmer without stirring. Continue to simmer over the lowest possible heat, stirring with a wooden spoon only once or twice, until the oats thicken, about 20 minutes. Add diced banana.

Remove the pan from heat, cover, and let rest for 2–3 minutes.

Pour prepared oatmeal into a bowl and top with Caramelized Banana, whipped cream, and cinnamon, if using.

# Granola

*This dish has been on the menu since we opened our doors. I love the smell of granola cooking in the oven. I love the addition of dried cherries; however, dried apricots, raisins, or cranberries would also work very well here. We serve our granola with Siggi's yogurt, but it's equally delicious with whole milk or almond milk.*

*Makes about 6 cups*

1/2 cup shelled pistachios

3 cups old-fashioned rolled oats

1 cup sliced blanched almonds

1/4 cup plus 1 tablespoon light brown sugar

1/2 teaspoon ground cinnamon

1/4 cup maple syrup

1/4 cup melted unsalted butter

1 teaspoon kosher salt

3/4 cup dried cherries

Preheat oven to 250 degrees.

In a food processor, lightly pulse pistachios for about 30 seconds.

In a large mixing bowl, combine oats, almonds, chopped pistachios, brown sugar, and cinnamon.

In a separate mixing bowl, combine maple syrup, butter, and salt. Combine both mixtures and divide equally onto 2 half-size sheet pans.

Bake for 1 hour, stirring and rotating every 15 minutes to achieve an even color.

Remove from oven and let cool completely. Place cooled granola in a mixing bowl and add dried cherries. Mix until all ingredients are evenly distributed. Store in an airtight container for up to 2 weeks.

# Vegan Banana Bread Granola

*This is a dangerous snack to have around the house. It is so good! We serve this granola at brunch with Chia Pudding (page 165) and fresh fruit for a vegan cereal bowl. It tastes and smells just like banana bread.*

*Makes 4 to 6 servings*

1 ripe banana

3 cups old-fashioned rolled oats

3/4 cup chopped pecans

1/4 cup turbinado sugar

1 teaspoon sea salt

1 teaspoon ground cinnamon

1 tablespoon chia seeds

1/4 cup coconut oil

2 tablespoons maple syrup

1 teaspoon vanilla extract

1/2 cup coconut flakes

Preheat oven to 350 degrees.

Mash banana thoroughly and set aside. Mix the oats, pecans, sugar, salt, cinnamon, and chia seeds together in a large mixing bowl.

Warm the coconut oil, maple syrup, and vanilla over medium-low heat in a small saucepan for about 5 minutes. Remove from heat and whisk in mashed banana until well combined. Pour over oat mixture and mix well.

Spread mixture evenly on a half-size sheet pan and bake for 25–30 minutes until golden brown, checking and stirring every 5–10 minutes. Add coconut flakes to granola for the last 5 minutes of baking. Store in an airtight container for up to 2 weeks.

# Lox Plate

*This is one of the signature dishes at the restaurant. Lox is short for gravlax, which means the salmon has been cured in salt. Curing is an old, no-heat cooking method. The salty mixture does its magic by penetrating the flesh.*

*Makes 1 serving*

>  A dollop of cream cheese
>
>  1 toasted bagel, of choice
>
>  3 ounces Beet-Cured Lox
>
>  1 tablespoon capers
>
>  Small handful greens tossed in lemon oil
>
>  4 to 5 thinly sliced red onions

*Makes 8 to 10 servings*

>  1 ($1^1/2$- to 2-pound) whole salmon fillet
>
>  4 to 5 sprigs dill
>
>  1 quart Beet Lox Cure (page 49)

For the perfect bite, slather cream cheese on the bagel, top with a slice of lox, and garnish with capers, tossed greens, and red onions.

VARIATION   For a vegetarian version, substitute a large beet for the salmon. Cut the beet in half and cure just as you would the salmon. Thinly slice and serve.

## BEET-CURED LOX

Place salmon on a cutting board and remove any pin bones with tweezers. Put 4 to 5 sprigs of dill and beet cure on top of fish, and wrap tightly 3 or 4 times with plastic wrap. Put wrapped fish in a baking dish and weigh down with a couple of cans of tomatoes or beans. Refrigerate for 3 days.

Unwrap plastic wrap and scrape off and discard dill and beet cure from fish. Slice salmon thinly and serve, or refrigerate for up to 1 week.

# Chicken and Waffle

*I know what you're thinking—fried chicken on a waffle? It sounds pretty crazy. In the South, we are all about it, and we serve a million of these at brunch. We use airline chicken, which is the breast attached to the wing bone. We brine it and dredge it, just like the Chicken Biscuit (page 76).*

*Makes 1 serving*

1 (12-ounce) airline chicken breast

2 cups Sweet Tea Chicken Brine (page 35)

1/2 cup Fried Chicken Batter (page 37)

1/2 cup Fried Chicken Dredge (page 37)

Canola oil for frying

1 prepared waffle, cut in half (see page 119)

1 tablespoon Sriracha Butter (page 69)

Pure maple syrup, warmed

Place chicken breast in brine and refrigerate for at least 8 hours (but no longer than 12).

Remove chicken from brine, rinsing off any spices or herbs, and pat dry with paper towels. Place chicken in a mixing bowl and pour the batter over it, turning to coat completely. Lift chicken out of bowl, letting excess batter drip off, and roll in dredge, pressing down on both sides so the flour clings tightly to the chicken. Let rest on a baking sheet lined with wax paper while you prepare oil.

Heat canola oil using a deep-fry candy thermometer in a large cast iron skillet to 275 degrees. Do not fill the skillet more than halfway with oil.

Gently lay chicken into the oil and cook for 6 minutes, adjusting heat as necessary to maintain 275 degrees. Flip chicken over and cook for an additional 6–7 minutes or until chicken registers 165 degrees.

Remove chicken from the oil and place on paper towels or a baking sheet lined with a wire rack to drain and rest for at least 5 minutes.

Place waffle on a plate and put fried chicken on top. Garnish with Sriracha Butter and as much maple syrup as you deem necessary.

# SIDES AND SNACKS

The recipes in this chapter are mainly what we serve to accompany our sandwiches or main dishes. However, they are also my go-to whenever I need a snack.

# Sautéed Kale

*This is one of the simplest recipes in the book, but it is also one of my favorites. Customers flip out over it. We let the ingredients do all the talking here, using organic lacinato kale, which is also called dinosaur kale, because it is sturdy and stands up to the high heat. We use refined coconut oil for sautéing the kale because it has a higher smoke point, meaning you can heat it higher than unrefined coconut oil.*

*Makes 1 to 2 servings*

> 1 tablespoon refined organic coconut oil
>
> 2 cups torn organic lacinato kale, washed and thick stems removed
>
> Splash of cold water
>
> Pinch of salt

Heat a large cast iron skillet over high heat. Just when the pan starts to smoke, about 1 minute, add coconut oil and reduce heat to medium high.

Add kale (you should hear the pan sizzle), and lightly toss with tongs. Let kale cook for 1–2 minutes then add water and salt. Once kale has started to wilt and water has completely evaporated, lift kale from skillet into a serving bowl.

# Coconut Curry Kale Greens

*I love the flavor of curry. This is a nice recipe if you want to give your kale a little zing, and it is amazing poured over Reggae Grits (page 143).*

*Makes 2 to 4 servings*

- 1 tablespoon refined organic coconut oil

- 2 teaspoons minced garlic (see page 34)

- 2 teaspoons minced onion (see page 34)

- 1/2 cup half-moon slices with skin on smoked sweet potato (optional)*

- 4 cups (about 1 pound) torn organic lacinato kale, washed and thick stems removed

- 1 teaspoon curry powder

- 1 tablespoon brown sugar

- Pinch of salt

- 1/4 teaspoon red pepper flakes

- 1/2 cup full-fat coconut milk

- 1/4 cup vegetable stock or water

- Chopped scallions (optional)

Heat a 10- to 12-inch cast iron skillet over medium heat. Once hot, add coconut oil, garlic, and onion. Sauté for 2–4 minutes or until garlic and onion are translucent and fragrant.

Add sweet potatoes, if using, kale, curry powder, brown sugar, and salt. Stir to combine and reduce heat to medium low. Cook for 2–3 minutes, stirring occasionally, or until greens are tender but not mushy.

Add pepper flakes, coconut milk, and vegetable stock. Stir to combine and cover to steam for 2–4 minutes, or until kale is tender. Taste for seasoning and garnish with chopped scallions. Serve immediately

*The sweet potatoes are optional in this recipe, but I love the smoky flavor it adds. If you don't have the time to smoke sweet potatoes, lightly steam or roast them. You want the sweet potato to be al dente; if they're overcooked, they will turn to mush.

# A NOTE ON GRITS

Before you take a stab at making grits—and I mean real grits, not that instant stuff (see page 20)—you need to understand that they take patience and will. Generally, grits require a 4:1 liquid-to-grit ratio, but once you add too much liquid, you can't go back. Do not add it all at once, but rather in small increments. Keep an eye on the grits, stir frequently, and taste, taste, taste. If you get to the end of the cooking time and the grits still seem dry and tough, keep adding liquid while stirring. The longer grits cook, the creamier they become, and that is what you want.

I have attempted to give you the best and most accurate recipe, but realize that if you've never made grits before, more than likely, you will not master them your first time. But don't give up!

# Broiled Cheddar Grits

*This is like the mac and cheese of grits. You can use most any melting cheese here, but we like sharp cheddar.*

*Makes 1 serving*

- 1 cup prepared Reggae Grits (page 143)
- 1/4 cup grated sharp cheddar cheese

Preheat broiler.

Place grits in an ovenproof bowl or ramekin, or, if you want to be super Southern, use a mini cast iron skillet. Add cheese to the top and broil on a rack 4 inches below the heating element. Broil for 2–3 minutes or until cheese is nicely browned. Serve immediately.

# Reggae Grits

*Reggae is kitchen slang for "regular" or "plain." Plain grits are good all the time—breakfast, lunch, or dinner. To me, there is nothing better than plain stone-ground grits cooked to perfection and topped with a healthy dose of freshly made butter and sea salt. Do yourself a favor and make the Mason Jar Butter to serve with this recipe. It is worth the effort—I promise!*

*Makes 4 to 6 servings*

- 1 cup white coarse-ground Logan Turnpike or other high-quality stone-ground grits

- 3 cups plus 1 to 2 additional cups cold water, chicken stock, or corn stock*

- 2 teaspoons kosher salt

- 1 tablespoon Mason Jar Butter (page 71), or other high-quality grass-fed butter

Place grits in a 4 1/2-quart saucepan and cover with 3 cups water. Using a whisk, stir a couple times to allow the chaff and hulls to float to the top. Skim off and discard using a fine tea strainer.

Turn the heat to high and stir like crazy to keep the grits moving until the liquid comes to a boil and grits start to thicken, 2–3 minutes. Add the salt.

Reduce heat to low until grits are just barely bubbling, and stir every 5 minutes for the next 30 minutes, adding additional water each time you stir if grits look dry. Cover for the last 5–10 minutes of cooking time until grits are creamy and tender.

Pour grits into a serving bowl and top with butter.

*Making corn stock is for sure a boss move. It's satisfying and even more amazing to cook grits in. Just heat water, covering corn cobs and onion, and let simmer for about 1 hour.

# Hashbrown Fritters

*I've never met a potato I didn't like. I first fell in love with potatoes watching my German nanny make pommes lyonnaise (potatoes fried with onions). Similar to an egg, the potato is a very versatile ingredient. These fritters are labor intensive, but you can store the potato balls in the refrigerator for up to 3 days before frying. We have served several types of potatoes since opening, but this is among my favorites.*

*Makes 10 to 12 servings*

> 5 pounds Yukon Gold potatoes
>
> 1/2 cup olive oil
>
> 1/2 cup minced onion (see page 34)
>
> 2 teaspoons kosher salt
>
> 2 teaspoons ground black pepper
>
> 1/4 cup clarified butter (see page 47)
>
> 1/4 cup blended egg whites
>
> 1/4 cup cornstarch
>
> Canola oil
>
> House Seasoning (page 50)
>
> Sliced scallions

Preheat oven to 375 degrees.

Wash potatoes, drain, and place in a large mixing bowl. Pour oil into a small mixing bowl and place it next to potatoes.

Put gloves on your hands, dip hands lightly in oil, and rub each potato, coating it evenly with oil. Repeat process with remaining potatoes and place on a full-size baking sheet, leaving about 1 inch of space between each potato.

Roast potatoes for 30 minutes until slightly soft. Remove from oven and cool. Place potatoes in the refrigerator for at least 1 hour before proceeding with the next steps.

Shred chilled potatoes, with skin on, over the largest holes of a box grater. Put shredded potatoes into a large mixing bowl and add onion, salt, pepper, butter, egg whites, and cornstarch and mix well.

Line a baking sheet with parchment paper. Using a 2-ounce ice cream scoop or a 1/4 cup measuring cup, scoop potato mixture and roll into approximately 30 balls. Place on prepared baking sheet.

Preheat oven to 200 degrees, Heat oil to 350 degrees, using a deep-fry candy thermometer, in a large cast iron skillet. Do not fill the skillet more than halfway with oil.

Using the palm of your hand, gently flatten 3–4 potato balls into fritters and place in hot oil. Cook for 1 minute, adjusting heat as necessary to maintain 350 degrees. Flip fritters over and cook for an additional 30 seconds–1 minute until golden brown.

Remove fritters from the oil and place on a baking sheet lined with a wire rack. Place in the oven to keep warm. Repeat with remaining fritters until they are all cooked. Season fritters with House Seasoning and scallions.

# Truffled Potatoes

*We serve these on our brunch menu. They are like potato skins with the flesh still inside. It's the perfect accompaniment to eggs or Ray's Waffle Burger (page 119). If you want to get real fancy, try these instead of English muffins with an eggs Benedict recipe.*

*Makes 4 servings*

- 2 large russet potatoes
- 2 teaspoons olive oil
- 2 tablespoons Maldon sea salt
- Canola oil
- 2 tablespoons truffle oil
- 2 tablespoons freshly grated Parmesan cheese
- Chopped parsley

Preheat oven to 375 degrees.

Coat each potato evenly with olive oil and rub with salt. Using a fork, pierce potatoes a couple of times and put in oven directly on the top rack. Place a baking sheet on the rack directly below the potatoes to catch any grease that drips off during cooking.

Bake potatoes for 45 minutes–1 hour until soft and tender throughout. Let cool completely and cut each potato in half vertically so you are left with 4 halves. Place potato halves on a cutting board or clean surface and gently press down with your palm or a steak weight (see page 25), lightly flattening the potato, being careful not to remove it from its skin.

Heat canola oil to 350 degrees, using a deep-fry candy thermometer, in a 4½-quart saucepan or large cast iron skillet. Do not fill the pot more than halfway with oil.

Gently lay flattened potato halves into the oil and cook for 2 minutes. Flip potatoes over and cook for an additional 2–3 minutes or until golden brown. Remove potato halves from the oil and place on paper towels or a baking sheet lined with a wire rack to drain.

Drizzle with truffle oil, Parmesan, and parsley and serve immediately.

# Bacon, Egg, and Cheese Deviled Eggs

*This is a fun brunch spin on a classic. We use bacon fat from Benton's Country Ham's bacon as it provides a punch of smoke. If substituting another brand, use a bacon of equal smokiness. If you can't find one, you can always cheat and use a dash (about 1 teaspoon) of liquid smoke instead.*

*Makes 12 halves*

6 hard-boiled eggs, peeled (see page 149)

3 tablespoons Mayonnaise (page 45)

1 tablespoon grated cheddar cheese

1 teaspoon stone-ground mustard

1 tablespoon bacon fat (see page 48)

Pinch of kosher salt

Ground black pepper, to taste

2 slices cooked and crumbled bacon

Minced chives

Using a paring knife, carefully cut a $1/8$-inch slice off of 2 sides of each egg and discard. This will ensure the eggs, when sliced in half and filled, will sit flat on the serving plate.

Cut each egg in half crosswise and carefully lift out the yolks, reserving whites, and place into a small mixing bowl. Add Mayonnaise, cheese, mustard, bacon fat, salt, and pepper to the yolks and mash with a fork.

Fill each reserved egg white half with a tablespoon of yolk mixture and garnish the tops with crumbled bacon and chives.

VARIATION  For a fun spin, try filling egg whites with Pimento Cheese Spread (page 82) and topping with Red Pepper Jelly (page 68).

# Classic Deviled Eggs

*Growing up, we always had these in the refrigerator for a quick snack. The deviled egg originated in Italy, but somehow found its way to the Southern dinner party. We serve them as an appetizer on our lunch menu, and like to come up with creative combinations.*

*Makes 12 halves*

6 hard-boiled eggs, peeled*

3 tablespoons Lemon Mayonnaise (page 46)

1 to 2 dashes Tabasco hot sauce

1 teaspoon prepared yellow mustard

1 teaspoon salt

1 teaspoon freshly ground black pepper

Paprika

Chopped pickles

Using a paring knife, carefully cut a $1/8$-inch slice off of 2 sides of each egg and discard. This will ensure the eggs, when sliced in half and filled, will sit flat on the serving plate.

Cut each egg in half crosswise and carefully lift out the yolks, reserving whites, and place into a small mixing bowl. Add mayonnaise, hot sauce, salt, and pepper to the yolks and mash with a fork.

Fill each reserved egg white half with a tablespoon of yolk mixture and garnish the tops with paprika and pickles.

*For hard-boiled eggs, boil eggs in water for 9 minutes. Turn off heat, cover, and let sit for another 2 minutes. If you live at high-altitude, you may need to boil eggs for 15 minutes.

**VARIATION** For a different taste treat, try topping the eggs with Beet-Cured Lox (page 133), fried capers, and a sprinkle of dill.

# Fried Pickled Green Tomatoes with Alabama Ranch

*This is a spin on traditional fried green tomatoes. To tell the truth, I never understood the craze behind fried green tomatoes, as they have no flavor to me. We use our pickled green tomatoes here, which pack a lot of punch, and serve them with Alabama Ranch (page 43). You could swap the tomatoes for pickles for another fun variation.*

*Makes 2 to 4 servings*

> 6 slices Pickled Green Tomatoes (page 38)
>
> $1/2$ cup prepared Fried Chicken Batter (page 37)
>
> $1/2$ cup Fried Chicken Dredge (page 37)
>
> Canola oil
>
> Salt, to taste
>
> Parsley, chopped, for garnish
>
> Alabama Ranch (page 43)

Remove tomatoes from brine and pat dry with paper towels. Place tomatoes in a mixing bowl and pour the batter over them, turning to coat completely. Lift tomatoes out of bowl, letting excess batter drip off, and roll in dredge, pressing down on both sides so flour clings tightly to tomatoes. Let rest on a baking sheet lined with wax paper while you prepare oil.

Heat canola oil to 350 degrees, using a deep-fry candy thermometer, in a large cast iron skillet. Do not fill the skillet more than halfway with oil.

Gently lay tomatoes into the oil and cook for 2 minutes, flip over, and cook for an additional 2 minutes or until golden brown.

Remove tomatoes from the oil and place on paper towels or a baking sheet lined with a wire rack to drain. Season with salt and chopped parsley and serve immediately with Alabama Ranch for dipping.

# PASTRIES AND DESSERTS

The recipes in this chapter can serve as a sweet beginning or end to any meal—or use them as a stepping stone to create something new. Try our Pastry Cream (page 162) as the perfect filling for a croissant or a topping to pancakes. Take Veronica's Cake Doughnuts (page 154) for a swim in your morning coffee, or try them in place of bread for a creative sandwich. Top your favorite ice cream with our Pie Crumb (page 165) or stuff homemade almond butter (see page 79) in between our Vanilla Wafers (page 159).

# Veronica's Cake Doughnuts

*Veronica helped raise my sister and me, and she was a phenomenal cook. One of my earliest cooking memories as a child was watching Veronica roll out and fry dough-nuts to perfection. As soon as I could see over the counter, I began assisting. To this day, when I smell these doughnuts cooking, I am transcended back to that kitchen with Veronica and reminded of the significant influence she had on my cooking. Before making these doughnuts, roll up your sleeves and channel your inner Veronica.*

*Makes about 1 dozen*

- 3 1/3 cups all-purpose flour plus extra for dusting, divided
- 1 cup granulated sugar
- 2 teaspoons baking powder
- 1 teaspoon baking soda
- 1/2 teaspoon kosher salt
- 1/2 teaspoon ground cinnamon
- 1/4 teaspoon freshly grated nutmeg
- 2 tablespoons shortening or softened unsalted butter
- 2 eggs
- 3/4 cup Banner Butter or other high-quality full-fat buttermilk
- Canola oil
- Confectioners' sugar

Add 1 1/2 cups of the flour, sugar, baking powder, baking soda, salt, cinnamon, nutmeg, shortening, eggs, and buttermilk in the bowl of a stand mixer and mix on low speed for 30 seconds. Scrape sides of bowl with a spatula, increase to medium speed, and continue to mix for 2 minutes. Stir in remaining flour and turn dough onto a well-floured board or counter. Roll dough around lightly to coat with flour to prevent sticking.

Using a rolling pin, roll dough to a 1/8-inch-thickness. Cut with a floured doughnut cutter—you should get 12 pieces.

Heat oil to 375 degrees, using a deep-fry candy thermometer, in a 4 1/2-quart saucepan. Do not fill the pot more than halfway with oil.

Slide doughnuts into hot oil with a wide metal spatula. Turn the doughnuts over as they rise to the surface. Fry until golden brown, 1–2 minutes on each side. Remove from oil and drain on paper towels. Serve immediately plain or rolled in confectioners' sugar.

# Cornbread

*In the South, cornbread isn't traditionally sweetened. However, I think it tastes better with a little sugar. I can already hear the disapproval from Southern grandmothers nationwide! At the restaurant, we bake all of our cornbread in mini loaf pans, but you can certainly use a standard loaf pan or large cast iron skillet.*

*Makes about 8 mini loaves, 1 standard bread loaf, or 1 cast iron skillet*

- $1/2$ cup (1 stick) European-style unsalted butter plus 1 to 2 additional tablespoons for pans
- $1/4$ cup whole milk
- 1 cup full-fat buttermilk
- 2 eggs
- $1\,1/4$ cups Anson Mills or other finely milled yellow cornmeal
- $3/4$ cup all-purpose flour
- $1/4$ cup granulated sugar
- 2 teaspoons baking powder
- $1/2$ teaspoon baking soda
- 1 teaspoon kosher salt

Preheat oven to 350 degrees, and grease pans with butter to prevent sticking.

Melt butter in microwave and set aside to cool. Add milk, buttermilk, and eggs to the bowl of a stand mixer fitted with the whisk attachment. Mix on medium speed until ingredients are incorporated, about 2 minutes.

Using a whisk, mix together cornmeal, flour, sugar, baking powder, baking soda, and salt in a medium mixing bowl.

Reduce mixer speed to low, add half of the dry ingredients to the milk mixture, and mix for about 30 seconds. Add remaining dry ingredients and mix until just incorporated. Scrape down the sides of the bowl with a silicone spatula to incorporate all ingredients.

Add melted butter and mix for 20 seconds or until butter is just mixed in. Pour batter into prepared pans, filling about three-fourths full. Bake for 10 minutes, rotate, and bake another 10 minutes. Remove cornbread from oven and test the middle for doneness with a cake tester or butter knife. If cornbread needs more cooking time, but the top looks brown, cover with aluminum foil and put back into oven until cake tester comes out clean.

# Vanilla Wafers

*Making your own Vanilla Wafers may seem daunting, but it is easy to do, and they are truly delicious. Creaming the butter and sugar is a very important step in ensuring your cookies bake at the right consistency. Important factors to remember when creaming are to make sure the butter is at room temperature and that you mix it with the sugar for at least 2–3 minutes until mixture is pale and fluffy.*

*Makes about 30 small wafers*

- $^1/2$ cup (1 stick) unsalted butter, room temperature
- $^1/2$ cup granulated sugar
- 1 cup all-purpose flour
- 1 teaspoon baking powder
- 1 egg
- 1 tablespoon vanilla extract
- 1 tablespoon whole milk
- $^1/2$ teaspoon kosher salt

Preheat oven to 325 degrees and line 2 half-size sheet pans with parchment paper.

Cream together butter and sugar in the bowl of a stand mixer fitted with the paddle attachment on medium speed until pale and fluffy, 3–5 minutes, scraping down the sides of the bowl halfway through with a silicone spatula.

Sift together flour and baking powder in a small bowl then slowly add to butter mixture, mixing on low speed until flour is incorporated. Scrape down sides of bowl again, return mixer to low speed, and add egg, vanilla, milk, and salt; thoroughly combine. Let batter chill in the refrigerator for at least 30 minutes before scooping.

Using a $^1/2$-ounce ice cream scoop or a tablespoon, scoop chilled dough onto prepared baking sheets, leaving a little space between each cookie. Use the heel of your hand to slightly flatten each ball.

Bake cookies, rotating the pans halfway through baking time, until golden brown, 12–15 minutes. Remove and let cool completely. Store in an airtight container before you eat them all!

# Mason Jar Banana Pudding

*Bananas are my absolute favorite thing in a dessert. I love them raw, cooked, or slathered on toast. We layer this pudding with several slices of fresh banana, Pastry Cream, and our fresh-baked Vanilla Wafers. We make these individually in Mason jars, but you could easily multiply the ingredients and serve them in something bigger if you wanted to feed a crowd.*

*Makes 1 serving*

- $1/2$ cup prepared and chilled Pastry Cream (page 162)

- 4 Vanilla Wafers (page 159), lightly crumbled

- $1/2$ ripe banana, sliced in $1/4$-inch rounds

- 2 tablespoons Vanilla Whipped Cream (page 104)

- 2 teaspoons feuilletine flakes*

Put a $1/4$ cup of the Pastry Cream in the bottom of a wide-mouth, 8-ounce Mason jar. Top with half of the crumbled wafers and all of the banana slices. Repeat with remaining Pastry Cream and wafers.

Top with whipped cream and feuilletine flakes.

*Feuilletine flakes are sugary pastry flakes you can purchase from most baking supply stores. I was introduced to them in the first kitchen job I had at One Midtown Kitchen. We used them to layer our iconic Kit Kat bar dessert, and I have been in love with them ever since. Corn flakes could be used as a substitute, but they won't be as good.

# Pastry Cream

*Pastry Cream is a wonderful base to have on hand for a variety of desserts and pastries. We use it to build our signature Mason Jar Banana Pudding (page 160), but it's equally wonderful on pancakes or tucked under fresh berries.*

*Makes about 4 cups*

1 1/4 cups granulated sugar

1/4 cup cornstarch

1/2 teaspoon kosher salt

4 cups half-and-half

4 whole eggs

2 egg yolks

1/4 cup unsalted butter

1 teaspoon vanilla extract

Whisk together sugar, cornstarch, and salt in a medium 4- to 6-quart saucepan.

In a large mixing bowl, combine half-and-half with eggs and yolks and add to the pan with the sugar mixture.

Cook over medium heat, stirring constantly, until mixture starts to thicken and boil, 5–10 minutes. Let mixture boil for at least 1 minute before removing from heat. Stir in butter and vanilla and whisk together until incorporated and shiny.

Pour pudding into airtight, nonreactive container and place a layer of plastic wrap over the top to prevent a film from forming. Refrigerate for about 1 hour or until chilled completely. Store in an airtight container in the refrigerator for up to a week.

# Chocolate Pancake Bites

*We use mini muffin tins to bake these, and they are really fun for kids. If you don't have mini muffin tins, you can use this batter to make pancakes.*

*Makes about 30 bites*

Clarified butter (see page 47)

1 recipe O.G. Buttermilk Pancake batter (page 92)

1/4 cup unsweetened Dutch processed cocoa powder

2 tablespoons sugar

1 tablespoon Espresso Powder (page 169)

1/4 cup semisweet chocolate chips

Confectioners' sugar

Maple syrup

Vanilla Whipped Cream (page 104)

Preheat oven to 350 degrees. Brush mini muffin tins with clarified butter.

Lightly whisk together pancake batter, cocoa powder, sugar, and Espresso Powder in a small mixing bowl. Using a silicone spatula, fold in chocolate chips. Chill batter in the refrigerator for at least 1 hour before baking.*

Pour batter into prepared muffin tins using a 1-ounce ice cream scoop or a heaping tablespoon. Bake for 10 minutes, rotate tin, and bake 5 minutes more. Let bites cool slightly before removing them from the tins, and serve with confectioners' sugar, maple syrup, and whipped cream.

*Refrigerating the batter before baking allows the gluten in the flour to rest, which will help it rise during the baking process.

# Chia Pudding

*Chia seeds are pretty magical and act as a natural thickening agent here. This pudding is amazing on its own or paired with our Vegan Banana Bread Granola (page 130).*

*Makes about 2 cups*

2 cups almond milk

1/2 cup chia seeds

1/2 teaspoon vanilla extract

1/4 cup maple syrup

In a medium mixing bowl, whisk together all ingredients thoroughly to ensure there are no clumps formed by the chia seeds. Pour mixture into an airtight container with a lid and store in the refrigerator overnight. The chia seeds will activate and expand, thickening the almond milk. Mix again in the morning. You should have a pudding consistency.

# Pie Crumb

*I am big on textures—I love crunch added to my desserts. We use this crumb to top our Cobbler Biscuit French Toast (page 96), but it also makes a great snack.*

*Makes about 2 cups*

3/4 cup all-purpose flour

1/2 cup granulated sugar

1 teaspoon cornstarch

1 teaspoon kosher salt

1/4 cup unsalted butter, melted

Preheat oven to 325 degrees. Line a half-sheet pan with parchment paper.

Combine flour, sugar, cornstarch, and salt in the bowl of a stand mixer fitted with the paddle attachment and mix on low speed until well combined, 1–2 minutes.

Add the butter and continue to mix on low speed until mixture starts to come together in small clusters.

Spread the clusters on prepared sheet pan and bake for 10 minutes. Take tray out of oven and break up clusters. Return to oven and bake for another 10 minutes. Crumbs should be golden brown and slightly moist to the touch.

# Chocolate Churro Bites

*These little babies are simply delicious, and a great use for your leftover pancake bites.*

*Makes 1 to 2 servings*

Canola oil for frying

4 prepared Chocolate Pancake Bites (page 163)

$1/4$ cup Cinnamon Sugar (page 168)

1 tablespoon sheep's milk caramel*

1 tablespoon Vanilla Whipped Cream (page 104)

Heat oil to 350 degrees, using a deep-fry candy thermometer, in a $4^1/2$-quart saucepan. Do not fill the pot more than halfway with oil.

Gently lay pancake bites into the oil, cook for 1–2 minutes, lift out of pan, and roll in Cinnamon Sugar. Serve immediately with caramel and whipped cream.

*We buy sheep's milk caramel from Dayspring Dairy in Alabama, dayspring-dairy.com. You can purchase direct from their website, or regular caramel works well, too.

# Cinnamon Sugar

*Cinnamon Sugar is a great thing to have around the kitchen. You can sprinkle it on your pancakes, use it to top buttered toast, or roll doughnuts in it. Whatever the use may be, it's a good thing to have on hand.*

*Makes 2 cups*

1 1/2 cups granulated sugar

1/4 cup ground cinnamon

1 teaspoon freshly grated nutmeg

Place all ingredients into a small mixing bowl and, using a whisk, mix together until fully incorporated. If not using right away, place in a container with a tight-fitting lid, and put up on the shelf.

# Espresso Powder

*Espresso powder is easy to make and delivers an extra flavor punch to desserts. Try using it in place of vanilla extract in our Pastry Cream (page 162). We use decaf espresso beans so that it is more kid friendly. You can buy espresso powder at the store, but why would you? It's so simple to make, and all you need to pull it off is a coffee grinder.*

**Makes however much you feel like grinding**

Decaf whole espresso beans

Place beans in a coffee grinder, select espresso setting, and grind until all the beans are pushed through. Store in an airtight container for up to 1 month.

# Espresso Brownies with Buttermilk Whipped Cream

*This dessert pays homage to a little Italian restaurant, Eno, where I used to work in Midtown Atlanta. We made everything from scratch, and I was always tasked with making our dessert brownies. These brownies were like nothing I had ever tasted before—they were moist, dense, and decadent. Everything we did at Eno was pure, and we highlighted ingredients in a way that let them shine. Since then, I have always carried around that brownie recipe, and over the years I have adapted it to be my own. I add Espresso Powder here and pair the brownies with freshly whipped buttermilk cream, a play on coffee and cream.*

***Makes 16 large brownies or 32 mini brownies***

1 1/4 pounds (5 sticks) European-style unsalted butter

1 1/4 pounds high-quality dark chocolate (72%)

3 cups granulated sugar

1 teaspoon kosher salt

2 tablespoons vanilla extract

4 egg yolks

8 whole eggs

2 tablespoons Espresso Powder (page 169)

2 1/4 cups flour

Preheat oven to 350 degrees. Line a half-sheet pan with parchment paper and spray with nonstick cooking spray.

Cut butter into cubes and chop chocolate into bite-size pieces. Combine butter and chocolate together in a medium heat-proof mixing bowl and melt over a pot of boiling water (double-boiler method). Stir chocolate and butter mixture with a silicone spatula until chocolate has completely melted. Set aside to cool while you prepare the other ingredients.

Add sugar, salt, vanilla, egg yolks, and whole eggs to the bowl of stand mixer. Using the whisk attachment, mix together ingredients on medium speed for 5 minutes.

Mixture should be fluffy and pale yellow. Turn mixer off while you prepare the flour.

Sift together the Espresso Powder and flour in a small mixing bowl. Slowly add to the egg mixture and mix at a low speed, until flour is just incorporated. Be careful not to overmix.

Pour mixture onto prepared sheet pan. Let batter rest for about 5 minutes before putting in the oven so that it evens out in the pan. Bake for 10 minutes, rotate pan, and bake for 10–15 more minutes until edges are set and middle is gooey but not raw. Let brownies cool completely before cutting. Serve with Buttermilk Whipped Cream.

## BUTTERMILK WHIPPED CREAM

*Makes about 2 cups*

- $1/2$ cup confectioners' sugar

- 1 cup heavy cream, 40% fat content

- $1/8$ cup Banner Butter or other high-quality, full-fat buttermilk

Sift confectioners' sugar into the mixing bowl of a stand mixer. Add cream and beat with a whisk attachment on medium-low speed until soft peaks form, about 2 minutes. Slowly add buttermilk and continue to mix for another 1–2 minutes until firm peaks form. Refrigerate while you prepare the brownies.

# LEFTOVERS

Leftovers have gotten a bad rap over the years, but the truth is that they have major potential for next-day flavor. I can't stand wasting ingredients, especially ones that you source locally and pay top dollar for. Here are some fun recipes we make using items leftover from the day's shift. I would think twice before throwing away that doggie bag; sometimes leftovers are just better.

# Biscuit Crackers

*We always have leftover biscuits at the end of the day, and even though we donate most of them to local homeless shelters, I really like to find creative ways to use the leftovers. These crackers are highly addictive and easy to make. Try them with our Pimento Cheese Spread (page 82), with your favorite dip, or on their own for an afternoon snack.*

*Makes 8 to 10 crackers*

>  1 O.G. Buttermilk Biscuit, preferably 1 day old (page 59)
>
>  $1/4$ cup clarified butter (see page 47)
>
>  $1/2$ cup Cracker Seasoning (page 53)

Preheat oven to 350 degrees.

Slice biscuit into $1/4$-inch-thick slices using a serrated knife. You should get 8 to 10 pieces. Lay biscuit slices out on a baking sheet and bake for 5 minutes, flip crackers over, and bake for another 5 minutes.

Remove crackers from oven and gently brush with butter.

Sprinkle the tops of each cracker with the seasoning, return to the oven, and bake for another 2 minutes. Let cool completely before storing. Store in an airtight container for up to 5 days.

# Beet-Cured Lox Chips

*You will need to invest in a silpat for this recipe. They are relatively inexpensive and turn any sheet pan into a nonstick pan. You can get one off of Amazon or the Webstaurant store. Just make sure you get one that is slightly smaller than your sheet pan.*

*Makes 10 to 12 chips*

> Skin, intact, from 1 side of Beet-Cured Lox (page 133)
>
> Kosher salt

Preheat oven to 350 degrees. Scrape all of the salmon flesh away from the skin and pat skin dry with paper towels.

Line a sheet pan with a silpat and place salmon skin on top. Lightly spray the bottom of a second sheet pan with nonstick cooking spray and set it directly on top of salmon skin. This will help keep the skin flat as it cooks. Bake for 5–7 minutes until skin is browned and crispy. Remove skin from pans and drain on paper towels. Tear salmon skin into bite-size chips and season each with a pinch of kosher salt.

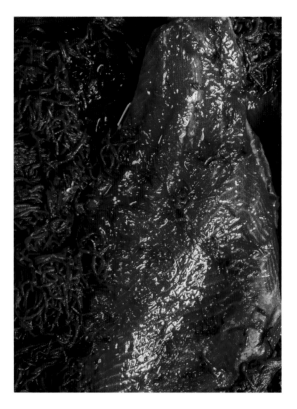

# Cornbread Croutons

*Croutons are always best when you use day-old bread. You can make any amount you want here as this recipe can easily be doubled or divided in half.*

*Makes about 4 cups*

- 4 cups day-old baked and cubed Cornbread (page 156)
- 2 tablespoons olive oil
- 2 teaspoons House Seasoning (page 50)

Preheat oven to 400 degrees.

Place Cornbread cubes on a sheet pan and sprinkle with olive oil and seasoning.

Bake until edges are golden brown, about 10–15 minutes, flipping over once during baking time.

# Cinnamon "Toast" Crunch

This is a fun spin on the breakfast cereal classic and a highly addictive snack. Tear day-old biscuits into bite-size pieces and deep fry at 350 degrees for about 1 minute. Roll in Cinnamon Sugar (page 168) and serve with milk or on their own.

# Twice-Cooked Bacon Jus

*This Bacon Jus can be used in a number of ways, but I like it best soaked into a piece of our Nashville Hot Griddled Cornbread (page 99).*

*Makes about 2 cups*

- 2 tablespoons bacon fat (see page 48)
- 1 stalk celery, minced
- 1/2 cup minced onion (see page 34)
- 2 cups small pieces cooked bacon
- 6 ounces lager-style beer, preferably flat
- 2 cups water
- 2 cups Chicken Stock (page 36)

Heat an 8-quart stock pot over medium-low heat. Add the bacon fat, celery, and onion and cook until the onion begins to turn translucent. Add the bacon pieces, beer, water, and stock, cover the pot, and lightly simmer for 1 hour. Pour the mixture through a chinois or a fine-mesh strainer, reserving the liquid. Refrigerate overnight.

Remove the Bacon Jus from the refrigerator, use a spoon to scrape off any white layer of fat that has solidified on the top, and discard white layer of fat.

To serve, bring Bacon Jus to a boil and reduce by half, about 15 minutes.

# Cold Fried Chicken Salad

*I personally love cold fried chicken, and chicken salad is a must in the South. We use our leftover fried chicken (page 76) in this recipe, as the breading provides amazing flavor and crunch.*

*Makes 6 to 8 servings*

- 1 cup Alabama Ranch (page 43)

- 4 cups diced fried chicken (see page 76), preferably 1 day old and cold

- 1 large stalk celery, minced

Mix all ingredients together in a medium mixing bowl and serve immediately on buttered toast or on a bed of greens. If you want to be extra fancy, top with a Fried Pickled Green Tomato (page 150) and a couple of slices of cooked bacon.

# Grit Cakes

*When you store cooked grits in the refrigerator, they thicken, making them easy to manipulate into different shapes. These grit cakes are awesome on their own or as a base for eggs Benedict or gravy.*

*Makes 6 to 8 cakes*

   1 tablespoon butter, room temperature

   1 to 2 cups prepared Reggae Grits (page 143), room temperature

   1/4 cup cornstarch

   Canola oil

   Sea salt

Grease the inside of a 16-ounce wide-mouth Mason jar with butter. Make sure you use a wide-mouth jar, otherwise you won't be able to slide the grits out when ready to slice. Fill with grits, cover with lid, and let set up in the refrigerator until completely chilled, at least 1 hour.

Pour cornstarch into a shallow baking dish. Slide grits out onto a cutting board and slice into 1/2-inch-thick discs. Lightly dredge discs in cornstarch.

Heat about 1 inch of oil in a large cast iron skillet until almost smoking. Gently add grit cakes to skillet, being careful not to crowd the discs, and fry until golden brown, 1–2 minutes on each side. Lift grit cakes out of the oil using a slotted spatula and set onto paper towels to drain.

Season with sea salt and serve immediately.

# Coffee-Sugar Face and Body Scrub

*We grind our coffee daily, and always have leftover grinds at the end of the day. Coffee stimulates the skin and increases production of collagen. I suggest using granulated sugar for the face scrub, since it is finer, and brown sugar for the body. What could be better than an edible face rub?*

*Makes about 2 cups*

- 1/2 cup coarse coffee grounds
- 1/2 cup granulated sugar or brown sugar
- 1/4 cup melted coconut oil

Place coffee grounds in a small mixing bowl and mix with sugar and oil. Store in your favorite glass jar or sealable container. Use within 1–2 months.

# Chicken Salad Fritters with Sriracha-Chive Aioli

*On Saturday and Sunday, we roll over to our brunch menu, so it's typical on a Friday to have lunch items leftover. One of my managers, Julian, had an awesome idea of dredging and frying the leftover chicken salad. The addition of bacon and paprika gives it a punch of flavor, and the Sriracha-Chive Aioli is the perfect accompaniment.*

*Makes 5 to 6 fritters*

> $^1/_2$ cup prepared chicken salad, of choice
>
> $^3/_4$ cup cooked and chopped bacon
>
> 1 to 2 tablespoons Lemon Mayonnaise (page 46)
>
> 1 teaspoon smoked paprika
>
> 1 teaspoon garlic powder
>
> Canola oil
>
> $^1/_2$ cup Fried Chicken Batter (page 37)
>
> $^1/_2$ cup Fried Chicken Dredge (page 37)
>
> House Seasoning (page 50), to taste

In a large mixing bowl, combine chicken salad with bacon, mayonnaise, paprika, and garlic powder. Using a 2-ounce ice cream scoop or large tablespoon, portion out chicken salad and roll into 5 or 6 balls. Place in freezer for 30 minutes before frying.

Preheat oil to 350 degrees in a 4$^1/_2$-quart saucepan or a large cast iron skillet.

Remove fritters from the freezer and put in a small mixing bowl. Pour the batter over them, turning to coat completely. Lift out of bowl, letting excess batter drip off, and roll in dredge.

Carefully place in oil and fry 1–2 minutes or until golden brown, rolling to fry all sides. Remove from oil and place on paper towels or a sheet pan lined with a wire rack to drain. Sprinkle with seasoning and serve immediately with aioli.

# SRIRACHA-CHIVE AIOLI

*Makes 2 cups*

2 cups Lemon Mayonnaise
(page 46)

¹/4 cup Sriracha

2 tablespoons minced chives

Whisk together mayonnaise, Sriracha, and chives in a small mixing bowl. Set aside while you make the fritters.

# DRINKS

Drinks are important, especially first thing in the morning. We serve all the usual options, but we keep it as simple as possible to not overshadow the integrity of the ingredients. You won't find an espresso machine behind our bar; we use French presses to turn out fresh-tasting pure coffee. Our mimosas are nothing fancy, but they are made with fresh juice we squeeze daily. All of the syrups used to flavor teas and lemonade are made in house with turbinado sugar, which lends a robust, unique flavor. Fresh cold brew and organic almond milk give our iced lattes personality, and glass-bottled sodas give you relief from a hot day. Whether you are a Bloody Mary aficionado or sweet tea fiend, we've got you covered.

When making cocktails, always use a cocktail jigger or shot glass for accurate ounce measurements.

# MIMOSAS

Just say the word "mimosa" at brunch and customers will line up. We serve a lot of variations for that reason. Important things to remember when making your own mimosas are to always pour the sparkling wine first and never stir when adding the remaining ingredients, or the mimosas will get flat. Make sure all ingredients are extremely cold.

# Classic Mimosa

*This classic brunch cocktail is the one we sell the most at the restaurant. The secret to making the best classic mimosa is to squeeze your own juice and use a high-quality sparkling wine.*

*Makes 1 cocktail*

> 5 ounces cold sparkling wine, such as Cava
>
> 3 ounces cold fresh-squeezed orange juice
>
> Orange wheel, for garnish

Pour sparkling wine into an 8-ounce champagne flute, top with orange juice, and garnish with orange wheel.

# Old Fashioned Mimosa

*I think an Old Fashioned is one of the best cocktails ever crafted. However, it's a hard sell during breakfast. We decided to turn this classic into a mimosa.*

*Makes 1 cocktail*

- 2 dashes orange bitters

- 1/2 ounce bourbon, of choice

- 1 high-quality maraschino cherry, such as Luxardo

- 1 teaspoon maraschino cherry juice

- 4 ounces cold sparkling wine, such as Cava

- 2 ounces cold fresh-squeezed orange juice

- Orange wheel, for garnish

Pour bitters, bourbon, cherry, and cherry juice into the bottom of an 8-ounce champagne flute. Add sparkling wine, top with orange juice, and garnish with orange wheel.

# Salty Dog Mimosa

*This is a play on the classic salty dog cocktail and a brunch favorite.*

*Makes 1 cocktail*

Kosher salt

5 ounces cold sparkling wine, such as Cava

3 ounces cold fresh-squeezed grapefruit juice

Lime wheel for garnish

Line half of the rim of an 8-ounce champagne flute with salt. Add sparkling wine, top with grapefruit juice, and garnish with lime wheel.

# MANmosa

*This is for all the men out there who think mimosas are too girly. No garnish needed here.*

*Makes 1 cocktail*

1 1/2 ounces chilled vodka

4 ounces cold fresh-squeezed orange juice

6 ounces local wheat beer, such as Scattered Sun or Blue Moon

Mix together vodka and orange juice in a cocktail shaker. Pour beer into a cold 16-ounce beer mug and top with vodka mixture.

# Margarita Mimosa

*We fresh squeeze all of our juices in house, so I highly suggest making the House Sweet-and-Sour Mix for this; it makes a big difference. The mix recipe makes a big batch—you can easily cut it in half or have it on hand. It will last up to 2 weeks in the refrigerator. If you insist, you can buy it at the store, but look for a local or organic brand.*

*Makes 1 cocktail*

Kosher salt

1/2 ounce silver tequila

4 ounces cold sparkling wine, such as Cava

2 ounces cold House Sweet-and-Sour Mix

Lime wheel, for garnish

Line half of the rim of an 8-ounce champagne flute with kosher salt. Add tequila, sparkling wine, top with sweet-and-sour mix, and garnish with lime wheel.

## HOUSE SWEET-AND-SOUR MIX

*Makes about 3 cups*

2 1/4 cups fresh-squeezed lime juice

1/2 cup fresh-squeezed orange juice

1/2 cup simple syrup

Shake juices and syrup together in a half-gallon jug or sealable container. Set aside while you prepare the mimosa.

# Milky Way Cold Brew

*This is a very popular cold brew drink we make—great for hot summer days. For a dairy-free version, replace half-and-half and milk with almond milk. Use a cocktail jigger to get appropriate amounts.*

*Makes 1 drink*

- 4 ounces cold brew concentrate (page 195) or store-bought brand, such as Califia
- $1/2$ ounce Vanilla Simple Syrup (below)
- 1 ounce half-and-half
- 1 ounce whole milk

Pour cold brew into the bottom of a 16-ounce Mason jar or large drinking glass. Add simple syrup and fill glass to the top with ice. Top with the half-and-half and milk.

# Simple Syrup

*We always have simple syrup on hand. It is very easy to make, so don't bother buying it.*

*Makes 4 cups*

- $2\,1/4$ cups water
- 2 cups turbinado sugar

Combine water and sugar together in a medium saucepan. Bring to a boil while stirring until sugar dissolves completely. Remove from heat and let cool. Store in the refrigerator for up to 1 month.

VARIATION For Vanilla Simple Syrup, add $1/2$ teaspoon of vanilla extract.

# French Press Coffee

*When I first opened Buttermilk, people thought I was crazy for serving French press coffee and said we could never keep up with the demand. We stuck true to it, and it is our signature way of making coffee. I always start my day with a cup of pressed coffee with fresh Vanilla Whipped Cream (page 104) on top. French press grounds are coarser and retain more of the natural oils than regular coffee grounds do. A French press also doesn't use a filter like the drip coffee does, which gives it a more robust flavor. Here's how to make the perfect cup.*

Preheat your favorite coffee mug and French press with hot water while you prepare the other ingredients.

Freshly grind beans of choice using a coffee grinder set on a coarse or medium setting.

Measure grounds using a 1 tablespoon ground coffee to 4 ounces hot water ratio, and add grounds to the bottom of the press.

Boil water and take off heat for 30 seconds. Pour over grounds in bottom of press, stir, and then cover with press lid.

Time for a perfect press should be right around 4 minutes. Plunge slowly then serve in heated mug.

# Cold Brew Russian

*This is a brunch play on the classic white Russian and will put some pep in your step. Our dear friends over at American Spirit Whiskey (ASW) helped us come up with this recipe, as it highlights their rye whiskey.*

*Makes 1 cocktail*

- 4 ounces cold brew concentrate*

- 1 ounce Rye Whiskey Maple Syrup (page 102)

- 1 1/2 ounces ASW Resurgens Rye Whiskey, or any other rye whiskey, of choice

- 2 ounces half-and-half

Mix together cold brew concentrate, whiskey syrup, and whiskey in a cocktail shaker. Fill a 16-ounce Mason jar with ice. Pour in cold brew mixture and top with half-and-half. Hold onto your hat and don't drive anywhere!

*Cold brew concentrate is easy to make by combining about 1 cup coarse-ground coffee beans with 4 cups water. Store in the refrigerator overnight or up to 24 hours. The longer it sits, the stronger it will be. Strain brew through a chinois or fine-mesh strainer into a container and pat yourself on the back for not spending four dollars on a store-bought cup.

# B.K. Bloody Mary

*Everyone loves a Bloody Mary. The most important thing is the mix. We use Sister's Sauce. This local company makes the best Bloody Mary mix I have ever tasted. Fun fact—the owner lives in my neighborhood; can't get more local than that!*

*Makes 1 cocktail*

- House Seasoning (page 50), optional
- 1 1/2 ounces vodka
- 4 to 5 ounces high-quality Bloody Mary mix
- 1 stick celery, for garnish
- 1 pickled veggie skewer,* for garnish
- 1 lemon wedge, for garnish

Line the rim of a 16-ounce Mason jar with House Seasoning and fill with ice. Pour in vodka and Bloody Mary mix. Drop in celery stick and use it to stir the mix a couple times. Add veggie skewer and place lemon wedge on rim.

*We make veggie skewers with 1–2 slices of our House Pickles (page 38), Pickled Green Tomatoes (page 38), and radishes, but you can get creative with your favorite combos. Try adding a slice of cooked bacon or pickled shrimp to boss it up.

# Sweet Tea

*Sweet tea is like water in the South. I was pretty much born with an IV of the stuff in my arm, and we always had a big batch in the refrigerator. If you do not like your tea on the sweet side, omit the simple syrup. You can also substitute the syrup with honey for a more robust flavor.*

*Makes ¹/₂ gallon or 8 to 10 servings*

¹/₂ gallon (8 cups) water

8 to 10 organic black tea bags

1¹/₂ cups Simple Syrup (page 191)

Lemon wedges, for garnish

Bring water and tea bags to a boil in a large saucepan, turn off heat, and let steep for 7 minutes. Discard tea bags. Add syrup and chill mixture completely. Once chilled, serve over ice with a lemon wedge.

# Lemonade

*There is something so nostalgic and American about lemonade. I think everyone at some point in their childhood operated a lemonade stand. In fact, it was my first lemonade stand that taught me how to run a business, minus the labor and rent fees.*

*Makes about 6 cups*

1 cup freshly squeezed lemon juice

1 cup Simple Syrup (page 191)

4 cups cold water

Lemon wedges, for garnish

In a pitcher, mix the lemon juice and simple syrup together until combined. Stir in the water. Serve over ice with a lemon wedge.

# The Arnold Palmer

*Combining the best of both worlds—tea and lemonade—The Arnold Palmer was the drink of choice of famous golfer Arnold Palmer and has become a Southern staple. Traditionally, the Arnold Palmer is 3 parts unsweetened tea to 1 part lemonade. Most people make it with half tea and half lemonade, which is a Half-and-Half. Some people also like it with sweetened tea instead of unsweetened. We Southerners can be very particular. We always ask our guests how they like it upon ordering, but my favorite combination is below.*

*Makes 1 drink*

> $1/2$ cup Sweet Tea (page 198)
>
> 2 to 3 ounces Lemonade (page 198)
>
> Lemon wedges, for garnish

Fill a 16-ounce Mason jar with ice. Add Sweet Tea and top with Lemonade. Serve with a lemon wedge.

# Strawberry-Iced Green Tea Latte

*Green tea is a one of those buzz words; you are beginning to see it more and more on menus. The taste can be slightly bitter, which is counteracted here by fresh strawberries and raw sugar. We use strawberries in the peak season, but you could also substitute cherries or blackberries.*

*Makes 2 to 3 drinks*

- 1 1/2 cups halved strawberries
- 1/4 cup turbinado sugar
- 2 green tea bags
- 16 ounces hot water
- 1 to 2 ounces milk of choice, such as whole, almond, or coconut

Using a big wooden spoon, muddle fruit and sugar together by mashing it in a small mixing bowl. In a measuring cup with a spout, combine tea bags and hot water. Let water infuse for 5 minutes then remove tea bags, pour into strawberry mixture, and chill completely.

Fill a 16-ounce Mason jar with ice to the top. Ladle in about 1 cup of infused tea and top with milk.

# Index

## Metric Conversion Chart

| VOLUME MEASUREMENTS | | WEIGHT MEASUREMENTS | | TEMPERATURE CONVERSION | |
| --- | --- | --- | --- | --- | --- |
| U.S. | Metric | U.S. | Metric | Fahrenheit | Celsius |
| 1 teaspoon | 5 ml | ½ ounce | 15 g | 250 | 120 |
| 1 tablespoon | 15 ml | 1 ounce | 30 g | 300 | 150 |
| ¼ cup | 60 ml | 3 ounces | 90 g | 325 | 160 |
| ⅓ cup | 75 ml | 4 ounces | 115 g | 350 | 180 |
| ½ cup | 125 ml | 8 ounces | 225 g | 375 | 190 |
| ⅔ cup | 150 ml | 12 ounces | 350 g | 400 | 200 |
| ¾ cup | 175 ml | 1 pound | 450 g | 425 | 220 |
| 1 cup | 250 ml | 2 ¼ pounds | 1 kg | 450 | 230 |